Nightmare in the Woods

One family's strange and terrifying encounter with Bigfoot in the Northeastern United States.

A.H. VERGE

ıtmare in the Woods

ily's strange and terrifying true
with Bigfoot in the Northeastern
United States

By A.H. Verge

First Printing: January 2017
Second Printing: April 2018
Copyright © 2017 by A. H. Verge

STONEBEAR PUBLISHING
StoneBearPublishing.com

Cover Design: Mark Johnson

Printed in the United States of America
All rights reserved.
ISBN 9 7 8 1 7 3 2 1 7 0 8 0 3

"Everything we shut our eyes to, everything we run away from, everything we deny, denigrate or despise, serves to defeat us in the end. What seems nasty, painful, evil, can become a source of beauty, joy and strength, if faced with an open mind."

Henry Miller - (1891-1980)

Dedicated to my Family

ACKNOWLEDGEMENTS

I would like to thank my wife Linda for her constant belief and support. Without her persistence, I would never have begun. I would also like to thank my daughters Elizabeth and Cassandra. They always remind me to look at life from a different perspective. In times of frustration and despair, they remind me what life is about.

I also thank Bonnie for reassuring me of my past through her own. Grace for her expertise in helping me through difficulties and of course my mother and father, for standing beside me and guiding me through a very difficult time in my life. Collectively they authored the book and were present during every memory.

FORWARD

The facing of one's fears is a turning point in every person's life. Facing my own and overcoming it is the moment in time that I truly hold with great reverence. I have battled my demons for the first half of my life and became cheated out of my precious youth. My life is now half over, and I am only now just beginning to live.

I believe that there are mysteries in this world that were never meant to be discovered. Almost every continent has some sort of "wild man" that has lasted the test of time. Whether it be the Sasquatch, Loup-Garou, Messing, Skunk Ape, Wendigo, Yeti, Yowie or a host of other numerous names, the result is always the same. There remains an ever-growing list of sightings that continue to this day.

Whether it be of ignorance to science or the grasping of familiar traditions that keeps me in awe of the unexplained. I will continue to be respectful toward nature and know the limitations of man. The boundaries being clearly set; I will await the outcome.

TABLE OF CONTENTS

The Summer of 1976	1
The Eyes	16
Tracks in the Garden	25
Our Casted Tracks	39
The Nightmare Investigation	50
Games on the Back Deck	61
Discovering the Nest	68
The Authorities Get Involved	75
A Close Encounter	83
Standoff in the Garden	92
Face to Face with a Nightmare	103
Moving On	108
All Grown Up	116
Camping in Lancaster, PA	124
A Picnic Encounter	129
The Nightmare Continues	137
About the Author	143

Nightmare in the Woods

in the

Woods

One family's strange and terrifying encounter with Bigfoot in the Northeastern United States.

A.H. VERGE

The Summer of 1976

The last day of school was coming to a close as I stared at the clock face above the classroom door. I had raced that expressionless face the entire year, and I was determined to win. Winning signaling the onset of swimming and kickball games, hot dogs and adventure, and ice cream drives in the back of a pick-up truck in the warm summer nights.

There are few moments that stand out for an eight-year-old on the calendar – Christmas (of course), Halloween, birthdays, and the last day of school. Only fifteen minutes remained; the loud tick of the minute hand announcing the death of another moment in time with the promise of summer just around the corner. Terry, the bus driver, would be handing out the *goodie bags* on the way home with the usual – a half melted chocolate bar, a pencil that must have been in storage for at least ten years by the condition of the eraser, stickers that had no business being in a goodie bag, and a small roll of NECCO candies. Life was good and had the promise of only getting better for the next two months.

My teacher, Mrs. Alden, was giving the usual speech: *Don't forget to read over the summer and practice your numbers so that you will be ready for next fall.* The low din of the bell started to grow along with the rustle of the captive students who could no longer be contained. Summer had officially arrived!

Life in northern New Jersey in 1976 was uneventful. The Bi-Centennial was in full swing with economic patriotism served in every advertisement. The movie "Jaws" curbed any desire to swim in the ocean, while "The Exorcist" tested our faith. The fear we experienced existed only in the theater and vanished as soon as the credits began to roll.

All was well in my world that summer, with the first order of business was to sleep in late and possibly walk down the road to Parrish's pond for fishing. My plan was to make 1976 a summer I would never forget. Little did I know that the events about to take place would haunt me for the rest of my life. If I did, I would have gladly remained in school.

The official summer day began on Saturday. The smell of bacon floated up the stairs and aroused the primeval senses of my brain. Although I had no intention of rising early, there was no resisting the temptation.

I descended the stairs to find my mother standing at the stove, working like a maestro conducting a masterpiece. My father just entered with a drained cup of coffee from the back deck, looking for a refill. We lived on our back deck during the summer. I could hear the familiar sound of my older brother Al's dirt bike running by the barn, most likely getting ready for another ride in the woods behind our house. The backyard consisted of an old horse barn, an above ground pool, a greenhouse, and a large garden on the hill that bordered the woods overlooking our house. Al and I had cut trails throughout the woods to provide a labyrinth of accessibility to our homespun adventures.

Breakfast went as planned, with my parents announcing they would be working in the garden today. Al's friend, John, would be coming by later to discuss the age-old controversy that all teenagers face – cars and girls.

"Hey D," said Al. D was my nickname, short for Dale. "You want to go for a ride before the Gooch gets here?" Gooch being John's nickname. I never understood where the moniker Gooch came from, but the name just stuck. Everyone I knew seemed to have a nickname.

"OK," I replied. "Does Ma and Dad know?"

"Yeah, come on."

I ran into the horse barn and retrieved my

helmet, which sat on the feed can of rabbit food. I hated my helmet; it reminded me of a bobble head when I wore it. Al had the cool helmet, which not only covered his ears but also had a cool rebel flag painted on the top. My helmet was painted ugly blue with a bubble face shield as my only protection from branches. Unfortunately, there was no protection from the ridicule that the older kids aimed my way when they saw me. Still, I was suited up and ready to go for a morning of raw, outdoor adventure. I likened the moment to that of how a hell-raising biker would start a ride into the unknown.

Al started the Yamaha with a kick, and I climbed up behind him on the seat. My arms wrapped tightly around his waist with the hope of not falling off, we started out of the barn and began ascending the steep hill with the garden to our right. My father had recently removed the rusty wire fence along one side of the garden to install a new one but had not yet begun the project.

As we continued to climb the hill, my parents waved their approval, and I could see my mother mouth the words *be careful* as we sped on.

Entering the woods always took on an air of mystery; you were never alone with the wildlife that enveloped you as you passed by. I could not help but feel that there was something very different about this instance. We pressed on, and I put the feeling behind me, passing it on as just a moment of growing pains and the beginning of summer.

We continued down winding wooded trails where the sun tried to reach through the majestic canopy of green to touch the earth below. White Birch trees bowed gracefully to our approach as if royalty were upon them.

I could see the clearing up ahead, and I knew where Al was headed – the infamous power line access road. Al could reach high speeds on the small dirt road that connected the electric sentinels that spanned the countryside. They almost resembled giant robots that had been left behind from a faraway world. The dirt road began on a small country road where there were no homes present and ended at a small bungalow colony that had burned down years ago, leaving just a shell of what could have been a vacation community. All that was left were some basements and a few structures, like memories that were lost in an instant.

The start to the power lines access road, on the way to the Burnt Houses.

Al began his assault on the deserted highway and climbed to speeds of more than thirty-five miles per hour; an incredible speed that our parents would of course never accept. As we continued in the direction of the "burnt houses" as they were known, I could not help but feel somewhat apprehensive. The thought of the ghosts that may reside there made me very uneasy. We rounded the bend and there they were, just sitting in silence awaiting our arrival. We pulled up to what resembled a courtyard between the lost homes and turned off the Yamaha. The moment of silence was appreciated, but our escape was now shut down. I felt uneasy and wanted to leave.

"Are you scared, D?" Al inquired.

"Nah," I replied, with the hope that I was convincing enough. I tried desperately to hide my shaking hands and breaking voice.

"Maybe we should look around a bit, what do you say?" asked Al.

I was terrified and said, "Don't forget the Gooch is coming." I hoped that would be a good enough of an excuse to resume our ride home.

"Oh yeah, we better get back," Al responded.

The sound of the motor turning over was welcome music to my ears. Al pulled the bike around, and we headed for home with a sigh of relief. As we approached the turn to pull back on the trail toward home, Al stopped the bike and seemed to stare at the road past the trail. Suddenly, Al was pivoting the Yamaha as fast as he could.

"Hold on," he yelled back, and I knew something was wrong. I looked back to see what Al might have seen and saw nothing. In an instant, we were tearing through the trails on our homeward destination.

Something was wrong. I didn't know what it was, but Al was not himself. Our usual carefree ride along the trails seemed different, as though some unseen predator stalked us along our way; awaiting the right moment to take the course of action needed to overtake its prey.

Securing the Yamaha in the barn, we both walked down to the house where our parents sat on the deck with the day's freshly picked vegetables. I went into the house while Al spoke with our parents concerning the ride. Later I discovered my concern was warranted; Al had seen something along those trails but had shielded me from what he'd seen.

The next day began like any other day: the morning ritual of breakfast and contemplation as to what would be the most enjoyable course of action. We discussed the previous day's excursion on the Yamaha and determined that Al had seen a large black bear on the edge of the power line road. The thought of a bear roaming in *our* space sent a shiver through my soul. Of course, with our new visitor about, all activities past the property line were halted unless Al was with me. I didn't understand why Al had so much authority. Was it just because he was a teenager? Did some hidden power descend and provide him with the knowledge of the ages? All I know is that he was my only hope of exploration past the boundaries.

"Why don't you boys give the motorcycle a rest for a few days," said Dad. "By then the bear will have taken off for better hunting grounds."

My first thought was, not a problem. Just then, Al broke in. "Dad, the sound of the bike will scare him off. Besides, the other guys are coming over to ride." By the *other guys,*

Al meant the band of misfits he would hang around with from the neighborhood; the same brain trust that would be first in line to laugh at the sight of my helmet.

The site of the original Burnt Houses
as it looks today.

I despised these guys. Collectively, they had the intelligence of a bag of mud.

"I still think some time off the bike wouldn't hurt," said Dad. "Besides I want to do some trimming around the yard today."

Hearing my father say those words sent a feeling of exhaustion throughout my being. My Dad's idea of trimming consisted of hours of pruning and hedge trimming. Al and I responsible for the cleanup, dragging huge piles of branches up the hill to the woods edge where the compost pile was would surely finish any thought of enjoyment.

"Dad, what about the guys?" protested Al. "They're gonna be here in a little while."

"I think they'll understand," responded my father.

The feeling of hopelessness was unbearable. Al and I slowly proceeded out to the yard and awaited the dreaded pole saw to arrive. My father arrived with not only the saw but with the hedge trimmer and rake. Truly, a bad sign for a sunny summer day.

Six hours of constant dragging and raking was like a sentence reserved for only the most hardened of criminals. Looking down at my hands and seeing the blisters would surely be enough for a reprieve of sentence with Dad.

"Dad, look at my hands. They are starting to bleed," I said. "I better go wash them off before I get an infection or something."

"I think they will be just fine," Dad replied. "It will toughen them up. You don't want sissyhands, do you?"

"No," reluctantly I agreed. Then I dragged up another pile of branches for compost. Every time I reached the woods edge, I would stare, waiting to see the bear that I knew was waiting to slap me with that huge claw-infused paw.

Al had kept scaring me saying, "They can hit so hard, I heard it took a guy's head off out west."

That was all I needed to hear. I was on high alert and ready for anything at that point. Just as I deposited my payload onto the pile, I heard what sounded like branches snap within the forest. I turned and displayed my Olympic debut as I bounded down the hill toward my father and safety.

Upon reaching my Dad, he looked up and yelled, "What's the matter?"

"I heard something in the bushes up there," I panted.

He replied, "With all the noise you just made, I'm sure whatever was there is gone." I'm sure my father thought his statement would have the effect of disarming my fear, but it did not. I just had the feeling something was wrong, and I couldn't shake it.

"OK boys, let's put the tools away and get cleaned up," my father said.

Music to my ears, to say the least. I was in the house in no time; but being the youngest, I became accustomed to waiting my turn. My father was first in the only shower in the house, followed by Al. I sat in the hallway awaiting my turn with my clean clothes in one hand and a clean towel in the other.

"It's all yours," Al said as he exited the bathroom. From the snicker on his face, I knew what came next. A cold shower. After a quick shower, to say the least, we were ready to go out for dinner. Tired and sore, but with an incredible sense of satisfaction and accomplishment, the family went out to dinner to the local diner.

The Eyes

After a long day of yard work, dinner was enjoyable. We all finished our desserts and looked forward to going home and watching television. "Mutual of Omaha's Wild Kingdom" was on and my parents wouldn't miss an episode. Our television was a twenty-one inch Panasonic; state of the art at the time. We even had a remote control (which consisted of me lying on the floor in front of the TV and changing the channels when asked). I hoped we would get back in time to watch "The Wonderful World of Disney", but knew we would probably miss it.

The ride home was uneventful and

somewhat relaxing. The sound that our 1968 Ford Fairlane made as it tooled down the quiet road seemed to enchant me into thinking we were gliding through a foreign land. We rounded the last corner of our road, ever mindful for the deer that were always present, yet surprised to find none this evening. In fact, there was no wildlife whatsoever. The familiar sound of the frogs and night insects were non-existent. My father slowed the Ford down to make the right-hand turn up our driveway. We would drive up the hill and turn behind our house. The woods behind our house loomed further up the hill, with the backyard separating the woods from our driveway.

As we proceeded up the driveway, my mother blurted out, "Look at the eyes!"

We all looked up to where she was pointing at the tree line and saw nothing.

"They were bright yellow," she insisted. "They just seemed to go back and forth, and then ran off to the right toward the garden."

None of us witnessed any yellow eyes or had any sightings of anything running toward the garden. The evening was warm and muggy at about nine o'clock, and it is hard to make out anything in the darkness.

The top of the hill where the creature was first seen by my mother. This is where the cast of the footprint was taken.

"It's dark out," my father stated. "How can you see anything at all."

"The lights," she blurted. "They lit up the eyes of something on top of the hill, and it ran off."

I felt sorry for my mother at that point. There was a little teasing to the effect of perhaps it was a giant groundhog, or maybe a crazed deer. She took our heckling with all the grace and dignity of a queen and ended the barrage with the simple statement, "I know what I saw, and that's it!"

At that point, we all knew we had pushed our assault to the limit. Any further teasing on our part was a suicide mission of extreme proportion. My mother was only four feet, eleven inches tall and we respected every inch highly. Her family was off limits to strangers, and she protected her children as any lioness might have protected her cubs. Even though we were her own, she would only take just so much before retribution was inevitable.

"OK, we believe you. But you only got a glimpse of something shiny on the hill," my father said. "We were moving, and the lights were only up there for a split second."

"I know what I saw," she snapped.

I can't speak for everyone at that point, but I was convinced the enormous black bear of my thoughts had arrived. I began having visions of how it would tear through the windows downstairs while we were in the false safety of our beds. Or perhaps he would be strong enough to rip through the side of the house. At every moment, the bear was not only growing in my mind, but it was also becoming immortal. The imagination of an eight-year-old can best any logic known to man. All I knew was that this was the end, and we were all about to be eaten. Where were Al's buddies at a time like this? Surely, someone could show up as bait to allow my family to escape the inevitable, but none were present. Usually, they descended on our family like a swarm of yellow jackets. They would stare at me, almost taunting me to join them outside and I knew it would end in a slimy, spit covered finger jammed in my ear. The dreaded 'wet willy.'

We all hurried into the house while my father stood vigil on the back steps staring up at the wood line. He took on the air of all the superheroes of the day in one person. He was larger than life and was not easily frightened.

"Are you coming in, Dad?" I asked.

"In a minute," he responded.

I was scared at the thought that the monstrous beast of my nightmares could, at any moment, take my father from me. I devised a quick plan that I knew would not fail.

"Mutual of Omaha is coming on, Dad. You coming?"

I knew this would work. To my glee, my father turned and entered the house, closing the kitchen door as he did. A wave of relief flowed over me with the thought that we were all safe in the house, and with a little luck the bear would move on. We nestled down to watch television, but my thoughts were miles away. Up until tonight, we had only Al's sighting. We now had the confirmation of my mother, which trumped Al's story because, not only was she a grown up, but also Mom. There was something out there, and all I could think about was the scene from the Jaws movie where people wouldn't swim in the water for fear of being eaten. Was this the beginning of a wasted summer? Would we have to spend the entire two months on high alert, ever mindful of our surroundings? The thought of it made my stomach ache – no more fishing at Parish's pond down the road, or riding the Yamaha with Al in the woods. The other kids in the neighborhood and I had already discussed setting up the tents for backyard camping trips. Would that be over as well? Something needed to be done and soon. Perhaps we could speak to a hunter to kill the marauder lurking around my habitat. There was much to be done if we were going to save summer.

"Hey, Dad?" I asked. "Is there anything that we can put out to keep the bear away from us?"

At that point, our dog Sally began to bark and growl at the bathroom window in the back of our house. Only fourteen inches tall and of the most vicious and ferocious variety, Sally was a Chinese pug that would take on the bear and tear it to shreds if allowed. Snarling and jumping, the bear's legs from the knees down were fair game.

My father was up in a shot and ran into the kitchen to turn on the exterior flood light that lit the entire back yard. My heart fell through to the floor when I realized he was opening the kitchen door to step out onto the back steps to investigate. I couldn't bear the thought of losing my father to this monster. I was terrified and pleaded with my father to return. He just stood there on the top step staring out at the yard. My heart just froze, waiting for the order to beat again. My father slowly turned and moved towards the doorway, and I knew this was the moment the beast would strike. I closed my eyes because I couldn't bear to see my father yanked away at the last second. The familiar click of the door confirmed that my father was not only safe but still mine. Yes, something had to be done.

The rest of the evening was less eventful, but all of us were on edge. It was one thing for the bear to be in the woods behind our house, but entirely off-limits to be near our home. The evening ended with Al and I brushing our teeth in the only bathroom, the same one that Sally was barking at the window. Of course, we stayed as far away from the window as possible and brushed as quickly as we could. We then raced upstairs to our rooms for bed. As I settled into my bed, I stared out the window of my room which overlooked our side yard. I felt safe knowing that I was high enough above the ground to allow safe sleep, but I still worried about my parents on the first floor. I forced myself to watch the darkness for as long as possible until sleep took over.

That night I dreamed of horrible encounters with the bear waiting in the woods. Visions of blood-stained fangs and enormous claws prevented any restful sleep. My only thought was why? It was my summer, and I deserved it. What had I done to warrant this circumstance from happening?

It wasn't fair.

Tracks in the Garden

onday morning came with the expectation of any other day. As I wandered down the steps, I couldn't help but notice that the house was empty; no familiar smells of breakfast cooking or the chattering of the family at the table.

I ran into the kitchen to find a box of Cheerios on the counter with a bowl and spoon awaiting me. I looked at the clock to see it was ten thirty. It almost seemed to be laughing at me for wasting so much time in the morning, using the precious summer time that was allotted me. I poured myself a bowl of cereal and milk. I went to the sugar bowl and glanced about to see if anyone was in view.

"Four," I said aloud. That was how many spoonfuls of sugar needed for this morning's breakfast. Even though my mother told me on numerous occasions that too much sugar would rot my teeth and give me worms, it was still a necessity to provide an enjoyable meal. Besides, I had young teeth, and they were strong enough for now. I would worry about the rotten teeth when I got old, like in my thirties. The belief in worms was ridiculous – how would worms grow in my stomach from eating sugar? There were no worms in the sugar bowl, and I sure wasn't going to go eating any worms. I took my feast out to the living room where I turned on the television to an old Abbot and Costello movie. Yes, summer was good.

As I sat finishing my bowl of sugar, Al descended the stairs.

"Where's Ma and Dad?" he asked.

"I don't know; I just got up, and there's nobody here," I responded.

"Well, I'm riding today. Wanna come?"

After the excitement of the previous night, I thought Al had totally lost his mind.

The house where the incident happened. The kitchen door is on the side, and the bank near the woods is visible above the car.

"Are you nuts?" I asked. "There's a bear in the woods that wants to eat us."

"Shut up, you idiot," Al replied. "Bears are more afraid of us than we are of them."

"Boys," we heard our father say from outside. "Come out here a minute."

Al and I put our debate on hold and went out to the back deck where our parents were waiting.

"Sit down a minute. Ma and I want to talk to you."

As we sat down, we couldn't help but notice the concern on our parents' faces.

"Your Mother and I were in the garden this morning, and until further notice we want you both to stay in the house."

"Dad, no," Al exclaimed. "I'm riding with the guys today. We'll be careful. Besides, the noise will chase any bear out of here."

"You're staying in the house, and I'm not saying it again. If you want to keep that motorcycle, I won't hear another word. Understood?"

Without a word, Al turned and went into the house.

"What's going on Dad?" I asked.

"Nothing for now. Just stay in the house, okay?"

From the concern in my father's voice, I knew it was serious. My mother also looked visibly shaken. I couldn't help but notice my father was wearing his revolver on his side. Firearms were not a big deal in my home; we grew up with respect and knowledge of them and were not surprised to see them. I was surprised to see my father wearing it because he was never bothered by anything in the woods.

Abbot and Costello finished, and we got about half through a Clint Eastwood western when my mother came into the living room. Al was visibly upset with the decision of being put out of commission.

"Your father wants you to come up to the garden for a minute," my mother said. "He has something to show you."

We had never been faced with a situation like this before. The whole thing was very odd. We trudged up the hill between the pool and the greenhouse to the garden and found Dad standing in the middle. The neatly planted rows of vegetables always amazed me with its uniformity. The miracle of nature left me dumbfounded. We proceeded to go to where our father stood between a row of cabbages and tomato cages.

"Come here," he requested. "I want you to see something."

As I approached, he knelt and pointed to the ground. I could see in the loose soil a strange track pressed neatly into the ground.

"What is it?" I asked.

"I don't know," he replied. "I've never seen anything like it."

As I stared at that track, I desperately tried to outline the bear track that I knew was there but had trouble seeing it. The more I scrutinized over the evidence of our guest, the more I noticed that it was less bear-like and more…human. At approximately twelve inches long, the heel and toes could be clearly identified. At four-inches wide, the track became even more human. The part of the track that stood out and made us all stare was the depth – an astonishing two inches deep. My father then brought our attention to another print a little further away. The new track was an incredible sixteen inches long.

"Remember what Ma saw last night?" my father stated. "Well, look at this."

He then directed Al and me over to the top of the hill on the edge of the woods where my mother stated she had seen the glowing eyes. The twelve-inch footprints were everywhere. We traced the tracks to where the individual had exited the woods and stood on the hill overlooking our home. The prints then ran in a circle twice and into the garden where the fence had been removed. We followed the tracks inside the remaining garden fence, as if the unknown intruder had become trapped in our garden. They then continued into what used to be an old pig pen behind the barn. Then the tracks became frantic as if the individual thought it was trapped and looked for any escape. The wire fence encircling the pen was only open in a small five-foot entryway. The intruder apparently became desperate and stepped on the wire fence containing the old pig pen, crushing it into the ground. An old rabbit cage was also crushed in the next step. Two heel prints could clearly be seen on the ground five feet away as if the assailant had jumped from the cage to the ground. The prints then moved back up the hill on the other side of the garden fence and back to the wild. The game had now changed.

I sat in utter silence trying to understand what was presented before me. There was just no making any sense of it. I now wished for the mundane thought of a bear on the hunt. My contemplation was broken by the sound of my father's voice.

"Until I can figure what's going on around here, there's no more trips in the woods unless you're with your mother or me."

We all stared at the line of strange, giant like footprints in the soil, knowing that just hours before we would have been face to face with the owner. I glanced toward the tree line to see if we were perhaps being watched by our unknown intruder. There was nothing, or at least nothing I could see.

"D," Al blurted out. "Let's see which one looks the best, and we can make a cast of it."

"Huh?" was my only response.

"It's gonna rain tonight; lets cast one so we can keep it."

"Okay," I said. We then focused our attention in the barn for some casting material. "I saw them use plaster of Paris on a show I watched about making casts of footprints," Al stated. "Dad, do we have any plaster anywhere?"

"All I have is cement. But if you mix it a little sloppy it should work."

Our materials gathered, we then began searching the tracks for the best possible print available. With the help of our parents, we determined that the best prints were where my mom first spotted the creature. The ones in the garden were off limits so as not to 'trample through the garden,' as my mother put it. The large print was not possible since not only was there produce involved, but the creature had also stepped on a hose. The tracks in the old pig pen were also out of the question. I was always under the impression that the old pig pen would house all the venomous snakes in the world. Not to mention an array of ticks and giant spiders that were anxiously waiting to sink their fangs into me.

The top of the hill would have to do for casting prints, so we set out to make our evidential soup. With the help of our father, we were able to get the right consistency to cast two footprints on the top of the hill. As we did so, we couldn't help but notice the similarities in the footprints to our own. The only discrepancies were, of course, the tremendous weight that must have been needed to press so deeply into the ground and the lack of any arch. Our minds were swimming in thought, trying to reach a logical conclusion to a mystery that would rival any Hardy Boys story.

With the coming of darkness, we gathered our tools and headed indoors. There was no chance that we would be caught outside with our new unwelcome guest hanging around. We covered the prints with plastic garbage bags to prevent any damage from the oncoming rain and checked for any other evidence that we could find. After a cursory look about the pig pen, we noticed that along the rusty wire fence could be seen long strands of muddy grass, hanging down like a type of witch's wig. After a more careful examination, the muddy grass turned out to be rusty brown hair approximately four inches long.

"Al," I yelled. "Look at the hair on the fence."

Al turned and stared at the clump hanging as if torn from the owner.

"D, go in there and get it before it rains. I'll get a jar down to the house and save it."

I'm sure the look on my face was enough to explain the answer to the feeble request. There was no way that I was about to step into the 'den of death.'

Between the snakes and ticks, not to mention the spiders that were involved, a resounding "No," blurted from my mouth.

"Come on," Al stated. "Don't be such a baby."

"No," was the only response needed from me as I slowly turned and headed for the house. Al, of course, was quick to follow, leaving our new-found evidence until tomorrow.

That night we all were on edge. Even though we pretended not to be concerned and disguised our thoughts with the current dilemma of "The Walton's", we were still very much aware of our surroundings. I wondered if the beast would return for a second visit. The immediate thought of locking all the windows and doors before bedtime raced through my mind.

"What about the prints?" I blurted. "What if it comes back and sees what we did and gets mad, it could ruin them?"

"I'm sure they will be fine until morning," my mother stated.

Still, this was our chance to get into the news; possibly making millions of dollars in the process. Visions of the excess money reared a smile that could have rivaled Christmas morning.

"Maybe we should leave the backyard light on or something just in case," I said.

"If it's going to come back, I don't think the light will make any difference," stated my Dad.

The next morning, I woke with no appetite at all. My mother was sitting on the back deck with my father while Al was still in bed. I walked out to the deck with the morning blindness that sleep will provide in the bright sunlight.

"What's everybody doing," I asked.

My mother was the first to respond. "I'm

going to can tomato sauce today." Her tomato sauce was famous and the smell of the fresh tomatoes in the kitchen was heavenly.

"I have some ideas about the prints we took yesterday," my father said. "I think it could be someone playing a joke on us or something."

Al's band of misfits immediately came to my mind. If they were responsible for what had taken place, they would surely be about to meet their maker when my father got a hold of them. Just then Al appeared for breakfast.

"What's up?" Al stated.

"Is there a chance that your friends could be playing a joke on you with the prints?" asked my father.

"I don't think so. I didn't say anything to them about what was going on. Besides, it doesn't explain what I saw on the power line road the other day."

"I don't have any answers then for what's happening," my father said. "The only thing I can think of is something like the

Jersey Devil."

I had never heard anything like that before. I thought the Jersey Devil must be the most terrifying thing ever, and all I could think about was scenes from "The Exorcist" playing out in the woods around my house. Fear was mounting and looked like it was not going to subside anytime soon.

Our Casted Tracks

ur casted prints were all we could think about. Did they take, or perhaps were they lost with the last night's deluge of weather? Al and I couldn't wait to get to the top of the hill to inspect them for ourselves. Of course, we had no inclination of going to the woods edge without our father present; we had to wait for him to finish his morning cup of life before we could go.

After a moment or two, our father realized that we were at our wit's end in anticipation so he put the morning brew down on the table.

"Ok, let's go check them out to see what

we've got," he said.

I was afraid to climb the hill, but found the courage through my father and even Al. After all, he was a teenager and had the authority to watch over me. I was glad they were both there.

We climbed to within ten feet of the forest and peered into the dark glen, mindful of what may be there. Al uncovered the first print to find that the cement had cracked in the night. Our hearts sank to discover that the print was lost. The other prints had been damaged by the rain, so our only hope was that the second casting had survived.

Al slowly uncovered the second casting and found that not only was it intact, but extracted from the ground much easier than the first. We had it; the evidence needed to prove that something was stalking our home. It was almost a feeling of great relief to know that, if necessary, our proof was ready for even the most hardened skeptic from the tabloid newspapers.

Our fortune and future were now on auto pilot. We just had to sit back and think of how to spend the money. These were the thoughts of an eight-year-old. There was no belief from any other family member that we could become wealthy from our new visitor, or so I thought.

We gathered up debris from the castings and noticed that there were more prints than we originally realized. After a more careful examination, we determined that our guest had returned. Even my father showed signs of concern as he scanned the perimeter for intruders. The air became cold, even though the temperature remained high. We began backing down the hill with an ever vigil eye on the forest edge. Once in the safety of our surroundings, we felt much more at ease. My father searched for answers to the questions that we had recently been dealt, while my mother busied herself in the kitchen with canning.

Al and I investigated the casting and were quite surprised to find the detail it contained. Five toes were easily identified. The heel was pronounced with an overall depth of two inches. The sides of the track were visible without any form of an arch. Al and I then concluded that if the large track was sixteen inches, and this was only twelve. Perhaps this was the track of a juvenile.

Our minds raced. Even though neither of us would admit it out loud, we were under the belief that we could be dealing with a Bigfoot type of creature. We decided that perhaps we should involve our parents with our theory.

"Mom, Dad; could we talk a minute?" I asked.

Just then both parents entered the living room and asked, "What's the matter?"

Al started with, "D and I were thinking that the more we look at the prints, the more it sounds like a mother and juvenile."

Al, then said, what none of us had dared to say, "We think it might be Bigfoot."

The statement was out, and Al and I waited for a reply to vanquish any thoughts of insanity.

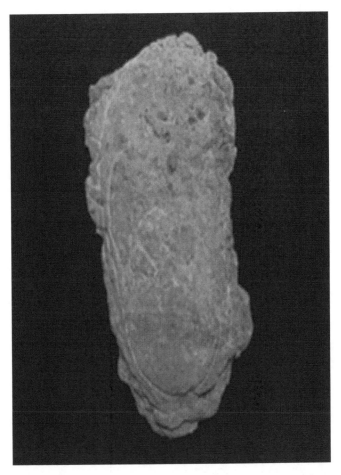

The original cement casting that was taken of a juvenile in 1976. The cast measures 13" long by 6" wide. It is also 2 ½" deep.

"I don't know what else it could be" my father said, which broke the heavy tension.

"I've hunted and spent many years in the woods, and I have never come across anything like this before. So you could be right" he added.

Just then, my brother's friend John, *the Gooch*, knocked on the door.

My father explained, "I don't think we should say anything to anybody right now until we can get a handle on this."

"What about Gooch," Al asked. "Can we at least tell him? He's like part of the family, and he's here all the time?"

"Okay," my father replied, "but only him, understood?"

"Understood!" Al exclaimed.

We couldn't wait to unload our new adventure on Gooch. We hoped that he would believe us and not think us totally crazy. However, he had hung around us long enough to know that we probably were.

As we explained to Gooch what was going on, he just sat in silence. I could tell that he was totally amazed and believed everything we said. I think the part of our story that convinced him was our evidential print that we obtained. He just sat there observing it and finally looked up with the most astonished look on his face that I've ever seen, and blurted, "Holy shit!" Immediately, he looked in my mother's direction for the swift justice that was surely on its way for swearing, only to be surprised by none.

"What are you guys going to do?" he asked.

"We don't know yet," I said.

"I'm thinking of setting a trap for it," Al uttered.

I just slowly looked at him in disbelief. My first thought was that he must be suffering from some delusional malady that had totally affected his brain.

My only recourse was, "Mom and Dad will never let you do that."

"Do you have any idea how much money this could be worth?" said Al.

I couldn't believe it. Al and I were finally on the same page. We could sell this and make a fortune! We didn't have to trap any-thing; we had the print!

Al interrupted my thoughts, "We either need the creature or at least a picture to prove we have it here, without a picture we have nothing."

"We have the print, I replied; doesn't that prove we have something?"

He answered, "Anyone can make a print, D. I can go make one in the mud right now of a dinosaur if it's a print you want. Now with a photo, that would be a different story!"

The thought of having to face this unknown creature made the hair on my head stand to attention.

"Gooch, you in?" asked Al.

"Sure, but what do I have to do?" asked Gooch.

Al replied, "We'll set up a trap to take its picture for when it comes back."

Feeling, unexpectedly left out I quickly stuttered by stating, "The first thing we have to do is get it okayed by mom and Dad." I knew it, I knew as soon as Gooch got involved; I'd be tossed aside.

"We is for Gooch and me, little brother; you're not part of the equation. Besides, mom and Dad will never let you do it anyway."

"That's not fair!" I shouted.

"I don't care what you think," Al replied. Shot down again, as always; I thought.

I then started to think about being outside with whatever it was lurking around our house, especially at night when it's dark and realized, maybe I didn't lose out after all and perhaps being indoors might just be the place to be now. After all, it was totally in my parents' hands. They, alone, had the power to approve this excursion or not. We all agreed that we would confront them with the idea during dinner.

"Ma, can The Gooch stay for dinner?" asked Al.

Mom replied, "If he wants to, he's welcome."

The stage was now set for the foundation of our plan. Dinner would either make our family rich or deliver us into a future of drudgery. Time would only tell with the hopes of great riches on all our minds.

As we sat and ate dinner, the Gooch and I wondered when Al would spring the question. If it were too soon, the plan would fall apart and be lost to the meal itself. If too late, we would be in the midst of being stuffed and not wanting to discuss it. It would have to be timed just right and worded accurately.

Just then my father broke in with, "So, what are you guys planning to do tonight?" It was as if he had already been privy to our plans and wanted to assist.

"We are thinking about trying to get a picture of what it is that's coming around at night," said Al. The Gooch and I were thinking of maybe sitting up late by the barn to find out what or who it is, so if it's someone messing around, we'll have the proof to show the cops.

"That's a good idea, but I don't want your brother up there," my father stated.

There it was again. I had crashed and burned more times in my life than a schizophrenic kamikaze pilot. Never in a million years would I ever be allowed to do anything or get the chance to be part of the investigation. It just wasn't fair. I would have to be content with staying on the "B" team and assist the "A" team when requested.

That was my only course of action for now, just sit and wait for my chance. Either way, it was way too late to get the articles needed for the plan to take place tonight. After discussing the matter with our parents, all agreed, tomorrow night was the night.

The Nightmare Investigation

My brother and I awoke the following morning with only one thought on our minds. We had to prepare for the assault scheduled this evening. The Gooch would be here this morning, and we would begin to gather the tools necessary. Half way through breakfast, the village idiots arrived from down the street with the hopes of riding on the trails. Leave it to these clowns to ruin everything.

"Hey, can Al ride today?" they asked my mom.

"Al has someone coming over in a little bit. I don't think he'll have time today. Sorry," my mother explained. The extreme pride I felt toward my mother at this point could have no comparison. She had single-handedly shut the morons down and sent them packing. Bravo, mom!

As I looked in their direction, I couldn't help but notice one of the boys placing his finger in his mouth and pointing it in my direction with a sneer that would make the very devil smile. All I could think of was, where is Bigfoot when you need him.

A few minutes later the Gooch came, and we began to plan our attack. I was surprised even to hear our parents chime in from time to time, assisting our efforts. Al and the Gooch were allowed to take pictures with only a couple of exceptions. They were to do it from the second floor of the horse barn so as not to be in the proximity to anything and they would also have to take a firearm to defend themselves, if necessary.

My parents' terms and conditions were agreed upon, so Al, the Gooch and I began by addressing the best place to get the picture. Since the garden area is where these 'beings' are attracted to, we all agreed that the garden would be the most suitable place. I thought to myself, was it the vegetables that attracted them or was it because, since the garden was nearby, it would have easy access to our house?

Al and Gooch busied themselves by, first running a flood light with an extension cord from a light atop of the horse barn. The second floor of the barn with its swinging door made baling hay more accommodating. However, that feat is now history. It now holds lumber and other materials. Soon it would hold sleeping bags, pillows, water and a camera.

While all five of us were sitting at the dinner table quietly and in anticipation, my mother was first to break the silence;

"I don't like this idea at all, not one bit!"

With that being said, Al and I began our protests at once until my father quashed the concern.

"He has a gun. And If I hear anything outside, I will be up there in a flash."

Earlier that day, my father furnished Al with his weapon for the evening. It was an old double barreled, twelve-gauge shotgun. That seemed to quiet the idea of this dangerous mission Al, and the Gooch were about to deploy for.

Deep down I had an urge to defy my father's word of caution concerning me and join Al and the Gooch that night. However, I knew that with the first sign of seeing or hearing anything creepy or inhuman would cause my bladder to fail me which would open me up to a lifetime of absolute ridicule.

It was seven thirty when we finished dinner, and it was starting to get dark outside. Yes, the time was right to start on this mission, but I could see a bit of reservation in Al's eyes as he headed for the door.

"If there are any problems, you yell, and we'll come up," Dad said as he left.

"Not one bit," mom bellowed.

We watched as they both went into the barn and the top barn door opened. I knew they were safe. The only way to get to the top of the barn was with the wall mounted ladder. Once up, one could close the trap door and contain the upstairs. My thoughts raced back and forth as to what the outcome could be. Would they get the picture and provide the family with riches? Would the creature even show up?

Still pondering the thought, since Al's room was double the size of mine, would I get a bigger room? All viable options to say the least. I guess I would have to wait until morning for the outcome.

That was the first night that I could ever remember where the television was turned off. My father and I played chess at the kitchen counter while my mother busied herself with the newspaper. In anticipation, we waited to hear the slightest noise of urgency.

Our dog, Sally announced that she had to go outside for her nightly business, but first my father set off to his bedroom to get his slippers. I didn't quite understand why since Sally was always permitted to go outside on her own, but my thoughts were laid to rest when my father came through the kitchen with a pistol in hand.

He let Sally out and stood on the back

steps as he watched the barn for any signs of a commotion that would lead him to believe there was a problem, but there was none. Sally returned, and they both stepped back into the kitchen. I caught a glimpse of my mother staring out the bathroom window as I passed by. The tension in our home was intolerable, and the slightest sound seemed to set us off into a state of panic.

It was eleven o'clock when we all decided to go to bed. I was exhausted. I would have to learn about the excitement of Al and Gooch's mission in the morning. As I laid my head on the pillow, I drifted off to sleep.

The next morning as I awoke, all I wanted to do was run downstairs to check on my brother and Gooch to see if they witnessed anything the night before. As I ventured into the hallway, I peered into Al's room and was stunned to discover that Al was asleep in his bed. Gooch was asleep on a cot on the other side of the room. My mind started soaring as to what could have possibly happened that led them to abandon their post? As I ran downstairs, I caught my mother in the hallway.

I asked, "What happened last night?"

"Shhh," she responded, "Your brother and John had a busy night. Come out on the deck, and we'll tell you all about it."

I followed my mother out onto the deck to find my father sipping on coffee at our redwood picnic table. The heat from the summer sun was already sweltering down upon us with the only shield protecting us being the blue and white umbrella in the middle of the table.

At this point, I was eager to learn what had happened to Al and the Gooch, so I asked again, "What happened?"

Dad replied, "Your brother and John had a visitor last night."

"Really?" I gasped. "Did they get a picture of this thing?"

Just then we heard Al and Gooch coming downstairs.

"Why don't I let them tell you all about it," said Dad.

As I waited in anticipation for them to

gather their bowls of cereal, they finally came outside. I couldn't wait any longer, so I demanded that they tell me what had happened! Al looked over at me, and I could see that his eyes had aged. He was not the same person he was before this occurrence. Will my brother ever recover from this phenomenon? I wondered. Even Gooch looked haggard compared to his usual self. I could only imagine that whatever they saw must have been awful. My mind raced with the thought that perhaps there was a near fatal attack and they nearly escaped the grips of this creature by the skin of their teeth! I wanted to know the details, but at the same time, I didn't.

Al and the Gooch just sat there eating their cereal; I couldn't stand the silence anymore and once again demanded they tell me what happened!

"Can I, at least eat my cereal first?" Al responded.

"No! I want to know now!" I replied.

Everyone was quite surprised by my tone or perhaps attitude toward this matter, and such behavior is usually taboo, but under the circumstances, it was tolerated.

Al finally broke the tension and told me what had happened;

"We climbed to the top of the barn. Everything was quiet; you could hear a pin drop. Then suddenly, we heard something coming out of the woods. We waited until we knew it was in the garden and hit the floodlights but they just flashed, and it grew dark again. The dew must have gotten into the sockets. So, we opened the door and looked out and saw a tall shadow in the garden. I think it saw us because when I moved, it moved.

It had quieted down for a while, but then we heard it breathing around the barn. This 'thing' was so huge, D, that it's breathing was so powerful! Something started to stink really bad, and we realized this creature must be here!"

"What did you do?" I asked.

Al continued, "Well we waited for that awful smell to go away and decided to get the hell out of there!"

I shot a quick glance toward my mom to see if there would be any retribution for cursing, but there were no signs of punishment on her part; so, the story continued.

"We came down the ladder with the shotgun to make sure nothing was downstairs in the barn. We didn't see anything but that smell came back, and we knew we were close to it. The Gooch followed down the ladder, and we slowly backed our way toward the house. We wanted to make sure nothing was coming toward us from behind. When we got close to the house, Dad was outside the door."

"That's when I let them in," Dad replied." It was about four in the morning. Our entire property reeked like a rotting deer carcass.

Al then continued, "We came in and told Ma and Dad what happened. You were lucky you weren't with us D because we would have slipped in the pee trail you would have left behind on the barn floor."

I waited with solemn vigil as the

laughing subsided and only thought how worried I was for my brother the night before. I should have just thought of that room change after all. All the night's excursion did was add credence to the fact that there was a creature very much alive in our back yard. We were questioning as to why it was there, what was its purpose for being on our property and when was it leaving? We were no further ahead than the first night the monster was seen.

Games on the Back Deck

n any given day, the usual daily routine would have consisted of working in the yard, along with spending time in the woods on motorcycles and setting up tents for camping in the back yard. But under the circumstances, there was no such thought to carry out our daily routines.

The only thought crossing all our minds was how to cope with 'the unknown.' Even the thought of swimming in our pool came to a halt due to the proximity of the wood's edge. Furiously, all I could think of was being cheated out of, what I had hoped to be the best summer of all. Instead, all we could do was stay close to the house and try to act like nothing was wrong, but that was hard to do, knowing all too well that this creature was lurking about and we still did not know what it was and why it was here.

Just then, Dad approached us and suggested we all go out today.

"Where?", asked my mother.

"Let's go for a ride and see where it takes us," said Dad.

According to my Dad, the idea of a ride was worse than any day of the *crazies*, which consisted of all of us piling into the car and driving endlessly in a random direction until night approached us.

The temperature was already reaching ninety degrees, and air conditioning didn't exist in our car. I usually sat behind my mother, but her window was always opened just a crack, God forbid the wind blows and messes up her hair; so needless to say, I sat there sweltering, guaranteed to suffer from heat exhaustion. Al sat behind my father who always had his window rolled all the way down, and of course, I stared at Al in envy.

"What about Gooch?" Al stated.

"He is more than welcome to join us if he wants," Dad replied.

My car ride just went from bad to worse. My seat now shifted from my normal spot to now over the 'hump' on the floor. Not only did I have to straddle this 'hump,' but I am now sitting between Al and the Gooch. I'm guaranteed over the course of this 'ride to nowhere' that it will consist of 'wet willies' and 'grinders.' I once made the mistake of asking them what a 'grinder' was, so instead of explaining, they decided to show me by placing their fist on my ribs and grinding back and forth to cause, not only pain but also laughter. I was doomed.

After spending the entire day roaming the countryside of Northern New Jersey, we returned home at around eight p.m. With no ribs left and with both ears dripping with saliva, my father pulled the Ford Fairlane into the driveway and our thoughts converted onto high alert. That anxiety fell upon us once home. We scanned the property in the darkness for our unwanted guest, but there was nothing. Could it be over as easily as it began? I could only hope.

The sky was clear and bright with every star hovering over our house, just waiting to be discovered.

Al interrupted my daydreaming by asking, "Who wants to play Monopoly?"

Music to my ears. Being that we lived on our deck during the summer, we often played board games outside by candlelight.

Within an instant, I was ready to play! After the money had been distributed, it was time to choose the game pieces. My first choice was the race car, but Al foiled it. Gooch snatched my second choice, the cowboy and of course, my father always took the top hat. My mother didn't join us but only waited for the usual argument to develop before intervening.

My only recourse was the stupid dog. A Scottie to say the least. Perhaps this is the reason as to why I chose a 'Scottie' as the family dog years later; I'll never know. Anyway, let the game begin.

We continued playing, arguing and scheming until the wee hours of the morning when my mother abruptly interjected; "Ok, time to head inside!"

My father agreed, "Yup, I'm tired, let's go."

The game was put away over my protest, leading me to believe that something was up. In an instant, we were all inside with our candlelight glow nothing more than a memory.

My father asked, "Is something wrong?"

Mom replied, "I thought I saw someone run across the field by the driveway." She continued with, "It looked like there was someone running slowly across the field toward the garden."

In an instant, the outside lights were on, and my face was pressed against the kitchen door window, searching the shadows for a movement to make sense of the situation. Dad passed me and stepped out onto the back steps. As the door closed behind him, I immediately smelled that vile smell in the air. This 'thing' was back! Our earlier expedition was in vain. My expectations dissolved like the fleeting summer wishes. Tomorrow would be the beginning of a new day and hopefully with it a solution.

The next day began like all the others. More questions than answers. My family was slowly breaking down as to how to solve this situation. We were all beginning to become on edge, so we decided that we cannot let the situation get the better of us. We will continue with our lives and not allow this "creature" to dominate our every thought. As a family, we all had certain routines to adhere by. For instance, one of our common enjoyments was to take long walks on the country roads in our neighborhood, but such distractions were not allowed at this time for fear of what might be awaiting us when we returned home.

If we could only outlast the intruder, then maybe we could have a shot of saving part of our summer. Our only hope was to outsmart "it" by staying indoors or at least remaining close to the house, and when the beast discovers that there was no way of achieving his goal of snatching one of us, he would be left with no other choice but to give up and move on.

It had to work; we just had to avoid venturing off into his domain. It was as simple as this; so, I thought.

Discovering the Nest

ad suggested, "What do you say we all take a walk today."

Of all the things I could possibly hear, that was a statement that tore my soul to shreds. It was as if they were looking to be attacked.

"Let's go!" replied mom and Al chimed in, "I'll go."

I thought to myself; it was over. There was no hope; we were destined to be preyed upon and destroyed. I waited and watched to see what direction my family would take for their walk.

I could have melted when instead they

began to climb the bank behind our house toward the woods. I could show no fear but still follow in anticipation, knowing this could be the end. I remember the look my father gave when he glanced my way. Perhaps it was the fear he saw welling in my eyes or the sudden lack of movement, so he steered my way to restore my faith, and that is when I noticed the glimmer of protection that was strapped to my father's hip.

His words burned a beacon of light into my mind as he bent down to whisper in my ear that lasted to this day.

He said, "Don't worry, I will never let anything hurt any of us, that's what Dads do, it's my job."

Although I knew if my Dad was with us, we were safe. However, I was still frightened. If our assailant was watching, he must be amazed at the lack of fear we exerted.

As we entered the woods, all we could hear was the sounds of the birds and wildlife, which was an indication that we were not being watched by our adversary. We continued down all the motorcycle trails as if we were gliding along on the Yamaha. We continued until we passed through the dark glen of leaning white birches, en route to the power lines access road. As the canopy opened, we could see the entrance way where Al and I had traveled just a few days earlier. It seemed as if years had gone by when we were safe, and the world made sense.

My family entered the power lines access road and continued down that one lane dirt road; still no signs of this creature, not even a glimpse of what's been stalking my dreams. As we continued, the forest seemed more at ease, as if there was more light than usual with an aura of peacefulness that surrounded us.

I continued to follow the group down the road when this feeling of ease drained out of me as we approached the burnt houses that I feared so much. All I could do was stare at the ghostly remnants of family memories that had been taken away so long ago. I stared through the emptiness of some glassless windows, waiting as to what could be staring back.

It was always an adventure when we traveled amongst the empty dwellings, trying to piece together the circumstances of the past. As we continued to walk past the display of debris strewn about the earth beneath us, we made sure to stop and observe every scorned bungalow in turn.

As we approached the largest of the abandoned homes, we fell upon some freshly disturbed soil around the walls that were left standing. My father bent down to examine the opening that once was a basement window and quickly stood back up. The expression on his face could have filled a novel! For he had the look of vigilance that immediately sent a shrill through my heart.

Without giving it a second thought, I had to see what my Dad had seen and when I proceeded to do so, I peered closely into the darkened chamber, and it all became visible! I first smelled that familiar odor and it was stronger than before. There was a combination of decay and fecal repulsion that permeated my nostrils and would have normally caused me to turn away, but I felt compelled to remain to assess the situation at hand.

I forced myself to look even deeper into this so-called abyss and there it was, in the very corner of the basement! I couldn't believe my eyes. It appeared to be a nest constructed of large amounts of grass and other soft materials. It wasn't like any other nest, for it was approximately a foot deep and eight feet long. We were all staring at the location where this creature took up residence!

Thoughts rushed through my mind as to how dangerous wild animals could be if they were cornered. Another thought shot through me like a lightning bolt – what if this creature was not only wild but had the capacity to reason like a human! The very thought terrified me!

Without another word spoken, my parents went into escape mode and guided us out of there as quietly as possible. We were on high alert to its fullest until the opening to the forest became visible.

As we walked through the woods, I took notice of the stillness that surrounded us. It's as if it took on an aura of a foreign land that was not apparent just a short time ago. No sounds of wild life to be heard, as if all the birds, insects and animals remained hidden, sensing that our stalker was nearby.

At this point, I felt we were being watched. I not only stayed very close to my father as we continued but also, I remained vigilant concerning the rest of my family. I thought, no one was going to be left behind, for we came together and we will exit this place together. The sky was beginning to grow dim. It was late afternoon, and we still had some ways to go to get home before the sun slumbered entirely below the horizon.

We were finally coming to a close as we approached the forest's edge overlooking our home. We finally felt more at ease. We were very close to reaching our domain when without any visible sign, that familiar odor took over the area. Our assailant made himself known to us, so we quickened the pace, being its unseen presence put the fear of death into us, speculating that at any moment we could be attacked by our predator.

We had survived the trip to the beast's lair. There are no words to explain this feeling of not only surviving this excursion but having all my family members return unbroken.

We survived but at what cost? We entered into the space of this unknown creature with no knowledge of whether they'll be any retribution on its part. We finally reached our deck and turned to see if we were being followed, but again, no sighting of it. We were home safe, and that's all that mattered.

The Authorities Get Involved

As we awoke the next morning; we were all under the impression that we had beaten the creature the day before. We decided we will not be deterred from living our life in fear. We felt empowered and strong, but soon thereof, we were proven wrong.

We discovered fresh tracks, not only around the garden again but closer to our house this time. It was if 'it' had become bolder as well. My parents concealed their fear very well so as not to alarm us but certainly showed their concern to this matter.

"I want you guys to stay in the house today" my Dad stated firmly. By the authority of his tone, we knew there was no debating his request.

He then went to the den where his desk was and skimmed through the phone book. The next thing I know, he was speaking to someone on the phone about the events that were taking place on our property. It puzzled me because we were instructed by our Dad not to discuss any of this with anyone. I let it go, figuring that he knows best and I was not in a position to second guess my father's actions.

I found out about an hour later as to who my father was confiding in as a Police car drove up our driveway followed by another unmarked vehicle. As the police officer approached the kitchen door, my parents were out in an instant before they had a chance to enter the home.

I tried to listen, but Al kept insisting I sit down and stop acting stupid about it. A few minutes later my parents returned and told us to stay in the house while the police officers were outside.

I looked out from the bathroom window to watch them search our entire property. They were taking photos and preparing plaster cast prints of their own of various tracks around the property. In just a couple of hours, they had prints, photos; they also took branches from various trees and a part of our remaining fence. For an eight-year-old boy, it was amazing to see how methodical they were with their tasks.

Once their job was done, they came to the door and handed my father a business card. I overheard one officer tell my father to call him in a couple of days to receive the results of their investigation.

I became excited, knowing these officers will have the answer to this mystery and we can, therefore, come up with a plan to get rid of this predator once and for all with the help of our Police force! This sent a flood of hope through me that I so desperately needed at the time. In just a few days, it was all going to be over with or so I thought.

My parents waited four days to place the

phone call to the acting police officer, even though we begged my Dad to do it sooner. However, he insisted on waiting an extra day just to ensure they covered all their bases to finally putting an end to this.

Once my father placed the call, he was left with more questions than answers. The phone number on the business card did not exist. Upon some research, there was no record of the police coming to our house at all. This left us extremely puzzled. We were left feeling alone with this along with no hope of help from anyone.

My parents became very angry, and I became scared again. Since my Dad concluded we were not going to get any assistance from the authorities, we would just have to deal with it ourselves. I came to realize that my Dad had every intention of shooting this creature to end this nightmare that we were all suffering from.

Several days had passed, and sightings of this predator seemed to have subsided. There were no tracks or odors to be endured. I thought, perhaps the authorities did do something to correct the situation but kept it from us or maybe, just maybe since we were so bold that day to venture off into its lair, it showed that we stood up to 'it,' forcing it to move on. All I knew at the time was that peace had been restored, knowing all too well, that it could be just a matter of time before 'it' would make itself known again.

As time passed, still nothing, I felt that it was finally over and there was nothing left to fear anymore. We began to live out our summer again, earnestly enjoying ourselves for the first time since school let out.

That evening there was still no sign of the creature. My family and I enjoyed the serenity of absolute peace of mind that even our killer pug Sally seemed relaxed. We sat and watched the antics of Archie Bunker in the latest episode of "All In The Family", and a sense of calmness enveloped us so that our atmosphere seemed blissful at last. My father was seated in his usual reclining throne cracking peanut shells between his thumb and finger while my mom was indexing coupons for tomorrow's trip to the grocery store. Al sitting in the dark hallway with the phone receiver glued to his ear, evidently speaking to some neighborhood rebel he associated with. I was stretched out on the living room floor with my pillow propped under one arm completely content with the thought of being safe.

The next morning, we seemed to have been back on track with our daily routines. My mother was standing at the stove conducting her breakfast symphony while my father poured himself a cup of coffee. Crepes were the choice of the day. Since we were originally from northern Vermont, crepes were a staple in every New England home. I patiently waited for my stack to be placed on my plate, Vermont maple syrup in hand; any other syrup would be considered motor oil in our home. As we all feasted on my mother's traditional goodness, not a word was said. The only noise heard was our forks anxiously scraping the plate for the last drop of that precious maple fluid.

After a moment of thought, I asked boldly, "Is it over?"

My father replied, "Yup, I think it moved on. We haven't seen anything for a couple of days now, so I think it's gone."

Over and finished! My summer can resume on track; the way I had originally planned it to be!

"Just for a couple of days, though, I don't want you boys near the woods just to make sure," suggested my father.

I guess staying out of the woods was a small price to pay to ensure this nightmare was truly over. Besides, a couple of the neighborhood kids were coming by later to ride bikes in the driveway. Perhaps this could lead to a kick ball game as well with the stakes being whatever dare we toss about to embarrass the other!

As I sat contemplating the day's events, my mother spoke up.

"There's a meteor shower tonight. Let's set up some lawn chairs on the deck so that we can watch it."

That sounded cool! It felt like such a long time that we were able to relax on our deck again without that fear brewing inside of us.

Yup, everything was getting back to normal again.

A Close Encounter

he night was warm and comfortable. I remember it being a Sunday. We had just finished dinner consisting of the usual hamburgers, hot dogs, hot Italian sausages, various salads and of course to top it all off, my mom's infamous fried zucchini and onions. I never understood the reason behind serving hot Italian sausage, though, but it goes to show you, grown-ups eat the weirdest foods. To complete this feast was my mother's famous iced tea. Everyone loved her tea. She would brew the tea bags, add sugar and one can of frozen orange juice in just the right proportions. Life had returned to how it should be.

We owned the first landscaping business in northern New Jersey, and we all helped out with raking and mowing lawns. Since my brother shared my father's name, "Al's Lawn Service" was chosen. The work was hard, but we enjoyed it as a family.

We all sat on the deck relaxing with the citronella candle glowing to keep the mosquitoes away, awaiting to watch the meteor shower, knowing all too well that tomorrow we would have to resume the family business.

Nighttime was approaching quickly and with it came the chirping of crickets along with tree frogs singing their song of nature. We set up our lawn chairs along with placing thick cushions on top to line our roost. The air was cooler this night, and a light summer breeze swept across our deck.

Our outside living room consisted as follows. The deck was eighteen feet long and eighteen feet wide. It was only two feet off the ground and had no need for handrails. Where the deck connected to the house consisted of the door leading into the den and a bathroom window. Opposite was a rock garden, and perpendicular was the driveway. Opposite that was a large hedge, and beyond that the large side yard where we held kickball games.

"There's one!" Al blurted out.

The show has begun. The stars were everywhere, and the long tails of our personal universal fireworks were amazing. Again and again, the skies did not disappoint us. We all just laid back and enjoyed our time together as a family.

We then heard the faint bark of Sally coming from inside. It sounded like she was on the other side of the house. We all just assumed she was barking at nothing.

As we continued to watch the Meteor shower in silence, we suddenly heard a sound of air dispelling from something. At first, we thought that one of us was sighing from excitement but quickly learned this was not the case.

The sound began to take on the rhythmic pattern of something or someone breathing, and it seemed close. It became deafening, so this was an indication that 'it' was now very close and along with this, the air changed rapidly. That noxious odor returned, and it was closer now than ever before. I glanced over at my mother and saw the panic in her eyes.

Al stared with his mouth open and my father, very calmly said, "Come to me."

My absolute fear fell back upon me, the creature of my nightmares was standing behind me on the other side of the tall hedge, although it remained incognito. Only two feet of vegetation separated me from this unknown horror. *It* was so close I could hear every cumbersome breath from our intruder, knowing that the fetid smell of its breathing was passing through its enormous teeth just a short distance from me.

I was utterly terrified! I looked in the direction of my father with high hopes that he had his pistol within arm's reach to aid me in time of need. Paralyzed, I could not move.

My father in his monotone voice, again stated, "come to me now."

I still couldn't move for fear that just

maybe it had not noticed me and that any movement on my part would instantly put me in a vulnerable position that would inevitably end in a gruesome result.

It was back and now within arms distance of my head. All I could think of was the size of the hands that our assailant possessed; perhaps large enough to instantly crush the skull of an eight-year-old boy. Again, I looked over to where my mother and Al were, in hopes that I could muster up the strength to speed jump toward them for the sake of my safety. But I was glued to the lounge chair with my legs crossed over one another.

It churned a guttural grumble behind me, and in an instant, my life light could be extinguished, and I'll never see it coming!

Before long, my father slid down to the bottom of his chair to a few inches from my feet. He wrapped his hands around my ankles and slowly pulled me toward him. I could remember his words so clearly some time ago, and it all came back to me at this moment, "I will never let anything hurt any of us." In my eyes, my father was larger than life, and I knew he would rescue me from this horrific situation.

I was beyond terrified and surrendered to my father's strength. Just then our dog started barking at the door just inches from my worst nightmare. Amid this frenzy, we turned in her direction and noticed the silhouette retreating from the hedge and retracing its steps back into the darkness.

Once this 'thing' disappeared, we all raced into the house. We were all in shock of the fact 'it' has now crossed the line. We felt that our personal space of security was assaulted. I immediately thought, perhaps this was some way of retribution for overstepping its boundaries by wandering into its own lair.

My parents became enraged! This 'thing' challenged their offspring, and this is one act my parents would not accept. It must be stopped, and this entire situation will have to end in the only way possible – it would have to die!

My father left the room only to return

with a flashlight and a loaded pistol. Seeing this, my mom panicked.

"Stay in the house! Don't go out there!"

Ignoring her protest, my father proceeded out onto the deck again. Our faces were pressed against the windows, watching but nothing could be seen since it was so dark out. We were only able to see my Dad's shadow with his outstretched arm, pistol in hand. Nothing, it was gone. I felt that it was confirmed that this thing came so close to home as revenge for stepping into its domain.

I sat and wondered how serious the next step would be and how long would it take before someone got injured or worse, abducted. An eight-year-old shouldn't have to live in fear this way, always wondering, always worrying as to what is going to happen next or what is this 'thing' and what does 'it' want from us? I felt it was time to make a choice as to whether I would be a wimp or a warrior, so I chose the latter. It's time to step up and never put myself in a position of being defenseless again.

Tomorrow will be the beginning of a new me and I will never be helpless again!

I woke up the next morning knowing all too well that there was a new challenge for us. We're usually awoken by seven a.m. to take on a day's work with our family landscaping jobs, but this morning they let me sleep in. Before I even went downstairs, it was decided that we would not be venturing off to landscaping jobs this day, but instead we were going to prep our home against the intruder.

My father and Al were already gone but left strict instructions to stay in the house until they returned. My mother and I stepped out onto the deck to examine the ground on the other side of the hedge to where this creature was standing. Once again, there were the deeptracks, and it was less than three feet from where I was sitting.

Once inside, it didn't take long until we heard my father's 1968 GMC pickup truck hustle up the driveway. I ran out to greet them and saw that they returned with a lot of supplies that would provide us with an advantage against this creature.

We put up flood lights along the driveway, hill, and barn and installed electrical wiring throughout the designated locations to where this creature lurks about.

All the while working diligently, I realized that we'd smelled the noxious odor, we saw the prints; we even saw its silhouette at night, but we never saw its face. Then again, would I want to?

Standoff in the Garden

ur home was now thoroughly turned into a fortress against the stalker. I couldn't help but think that perhaps it was becoming more of a prison than a house. Dad and Al installed flood lights that would cover the driveway, the hill, and barn. Shrubbery and other high vegetation were cut back to prevent anything from hiding in the shadows. Flashlights were made at the ready near windows, and of course, my father kept his pistol close to hand. There was also a 10-gauge shotgun that was carefully placed near the door exiting onto the deck. The trap was now set, and all that was left was to await our guest.

In some way, I felt sorry for the creature because I couldn't help but think of the pain that Dad would inflict upon it. Foolishness at its best. The creature must be stopped and eliminated if we were ever going to have peace again.

Sally the Pug jumped to her feet. We obtained 'Sally' from an article in the paper, and she was already named. We just figured that we shouldn't change her name even though it did cause some controversy with some of the neighbors. Unknown to my family, 'Sally' was also the name of a visiting relative at the neighbor's house. When we began to call Sally in from doing her business, it was thought we were mocking the elderly woman. It took finesse on my parent's part to explain that the kids meant no harm and eventually Sally was introduced to Sally. I preferred the Pug.

So, Sally was on her feet and staring toward the deck. I likened the movement to a well-trained military team. Flood lights were switched on, and flashlights were in hand. Each window shade was carefully opened to view the outside. Nothing. Almost in unison, all members of our elite group turned to view Sally sitting in the hallway with her head cocked to one side. I believe we all felt a little stupid, but after the recent events, it was warranted.

The evening passed without any further incident. All of us were on edge, to say the least.

"Bedtime," announced mom.

Usually, it would result in the standard, "Just a couple of more minutes," or "I'm hungry." When we tried to draw attention away from the moment, we would say; "I just want a drink of water."

That would buy us roughly five minutes of distraction, and if played right, that could easily be parlayed into an extra half an hour of TV time. That was not working right now.

Without anything else being said, Al and I merely climbed upstairs to our rooms. I had two windows that overlooked the side yard. The beast would have been standing below my window when it was watching me on the deck. I felt very uneasy. I pulled the curtains away from the window nearest my bed and stared out into the emptiness.

Where was it? Why couldn't it just leave and let us be? I just wanted to enjoy my time away from school before it was too late. I couldn't sleep. I didn't know if I was too scared or perhaps angry for what I had lost. It was not until later I would realize the depth of that question.

I slowly made my way across the hall to Al's room. Standing there in the doorway, I listened to see if Al was sleeping.

"What's the matter, D?" asked Al.

"I can't sleep," was my response.

I could just barely see by the moonlight streaming in from the window that Al merely pulled the covers back. It was all the invitation I needed to put aside my fear and crawl into the safety of my big brother's bed. I knew I would not have to fear while Al watched over me. I could feel all the anxiety and fatigue leave me as my head rested on the pillow. Even though the summer evening was warm, a blanket was needed, possibly for nothing more than an extra layer of protection against our intruder. I just lied there staring at the posters and pennants that Al had placed around his room. Lake George, New York, Vermont, New Hampshire. I'm safe. The visions became darkened as I slipped away for the first sound sleep in what felt like years.

I awoke staring into the eyes of the Wolf man. Al had collected various movie monster models and displayed them like trophies upon his dresser. Frankenstein, Godzilla, The Mummy, King Kong and even the Forgotten Prisoner. I couldn't stop staring at the Wolf man. I just stared and thought about our 'monster' lurking about our home. I carefully placed a T-shirt over the plastic menace in hopes that maybe, just maybe it would be that easy. The rationale of an eight-year-old.

I dressed and stumbled down the stairs into the kitchen. Al and my Dad had already left for the day, continuing with the family's business. Mom was busying herself on the deck with newly picked tomatoes for a fresh batch of tomato sauce. As I ventured out into the sunlight, the first thought was that the light would keep away the 'Boogeyman'. I didn't know, but it was a thought.

"D, would you give me a hand in a bit?" asked mom.

"What do you need?" I replied.

She stated, "I'm going to do some work in the garden and could use a hand."

The feeling gripped me to the core. The garden was only ten to twelve feet from the wood's edge. This couldn't happen! Dad was not home, and I was not allowed even to touch the pistol. I knew where it was but was given strict instructions never to touch the pistol or even look at it unless my Dad was with me. Now I was scared and had no clue as to what to do.

"Are you coming?" she asked.

Frantically I took matters into my hands. Al and I were given a metal 'pop' gun a few years earlier. They couldn't shoot anything, but we discovered that they could discharge a large amount of air and it sounded, surprisingly, like a gun blast. We had also discovered that by jamming the muzzle of the firearm into the dirt, it would shoot the dirt out for as much as fifteen feet. It wasn't much, but it was something. My only form of defense for myself and my mother. Dad wasn't home so I would have to assume the mantle of protector of the family.

"Coming!" I yelled back.

In an instant, the trusty piece was in my hand, and I was heading up the hill to the garden with my mother. This was either the bravest or dumbest thing I had ever done.

As we approached the garden, I could see the distinct lines of perfection in the rows of vegetables. It still amazes me to this day, the miracle of it all.

The garden was quiet, and my mother insisted she would only be a few minutes. With the old milk crate in tow, she proceeded to gather the necessary produce needed for her masterpiece. I, searching the area, discovered an old bucket that could easily act as a sniper's perch. I was ready, even though in the back of my mind I wanted nothing to do with any chance encounters.

I sat there quietly checking to ensure my

weapon was primed with fresh soil for a readied response. Not a sound was heard in any direction. As I glanced at my mother, her payload full, she busied herself with picking weeds between the rows. Just then, without the slightest bit of warning, a rock landed approximately ten feet from the two of us. I stared at the missile as if it was a foreign spacecraft landing. I slowly raised my eyes toward the woods and saw nothing.

As I whispered to my mom, "Did you see that?"

She looked up from her chore and said, "See what?"

"A rock just landed in the garden," I stated.

At this point, she stood upright and watched for a few minutes only to have nothing happen. She resumed her work, and I felt a little foolish, but I knew something was amiss. I clutched the toy a little tighter and could feel the cool steel in my grip.

As I carefully studied the terrain, another rock, larger in size, landed between my mother and me. My mother stopped and stared at the object, unable to say a word. She pretended not to let it worry her, but I believe to this day, she was terrified.

Then the unspeakable happened. She continued to weed the garden. My only thought was to get the hell out of there, but she stayed in defiance of the assault, not giving in. I pleaded with her to retreat, but she stayed. In total, five rocks were thrown in our direction.

Just then, fear gripped me harder than anything to date. What if the creature was male and wanted to abduct my mother? I flashed to the old "King Kong" movies and began to sweat. The monster fell in love with the lady and captured her! This was not going to happen! I leveled the barrel of my weapon to the woods and decided to show this perpetrator I was not one to mess with!

In an instant, the entire soil charge, in a loud bang, was emptied into the dense forest. I could hear the contents penetrating through the leaves and falling to the ground.

My mother jumped and yelled, "What did you do that for?"

I responded, "Let's go ma, I'm scared and I want to go back up into the house!"

Before my mother could answer, another rock landed only a few feet away from me. As my mom looked at the stone, it was decided it would be best to leave. As I bent down to pick up the crate, I handed my mother the weapon and began to carry the payload of freshly picked tomatoes. Just then, the bushes on the wood's edge exploded with activity. We need not look back because I knew this thing was coming for us.

We both ran down the small path to our deck and into the house. Remarkably not losing a single specimen, we were in the house in a shot! While catching my breath, my mom secured the doors and appeared with the pistol. We set up vigil at the window and watched to see if the creature dared to show itself in the daylight. Nothing. It was as if it was toying with us. Regardless, we stayed inside until my father and Al returned.

Even though my mother showed un-believable bravery, as my father walked through the door, she broke down sobbing. She began telling the tale that had unfolded, to my father. It was getting too close.

Face to Face
with a Nightmare

The events that took place in the garden only solidified the belief that we must not venture out alone. We had no idea what to expect from such a creature, nor its habits or its prey so that we couldn't take that chance.

For almost a week, there were no incidents and our family began to loosen the restrictions and once again, started to live as a normal family. We were still not permitted to discuss the events with anyone for fear of being ridiculed, so we thought it best to just let it go.

The entire air around our home had somehow changed. You could just tell that the creature had moved on to better ground. I was still having nightmares, but for the most part, it was over. We all believed it was finally gone. I can still remember the evening like it just happened. The summer night was very warm and humid. Fans were a staple in our house because we did not have air conditioning at the time. Now that danger had passed, windows were opened to allow fresh air to blow through the house; it felt good!

Everyone was at ease, and we just sat as a family watching television. I distinctly remember my father eating a dish of ice cream while relaxing in his recliner. This is how summer is supposed to be. As the time got on, we slowly started to head for our beds. Our home was a Cape Cod style house. It was small and sometimes cramped, but it felt comfortable. Al and I had our bedrooms upstairs, and my folks had theirs on the main floor. We only had one bathroom of course, and it was also downstairs.

Sometime during the night, I awoke with the need to attend to nature's calling. I recall how I slowly descended the stairs and found that the night light we had in our living room had gone out. With all the drama that had taken place, it left me a little rattled to enter a quiet, dark room. I proceeded to the bathroom and turned on the light. As the light touched every corner of the room, I could see that the bathroom window shade was up and the window was wide open.

Standing there before me was the face of my nightmare. I froze in absolute horror staring at the darkened face of our intruder. Its heavy round face resembled a combination of a primitive man and that of a Chimp, but much larger. I could see the darkened eye shine, staring at me for an eternity! I could not move. I only stood there watching every movement and crease of the face until the thought occurred that I am within five feet of this animal. I did not know what to do. Should I scream and wake everyone or should I simply stand my ground?

105

My decision was chosen for me because I could not utter a sound. I could only stare back at my nightmare and hope that it would leave! It stared at me long enough to almost acknowledge it had seen me and me, it. Then it slowly stepped to the side and out of sight. I stood there for a few more moments and then raised my hand and shut the lights. I could do nothing more. I also could not relieve my bladder. I had no intention of getting any closer to the window than I already had. I merely turned and went back upstairs.

I spent the rest of the night sitting on the side of my bed. I contemplated what I should do and formulated the plan. If there were no more incidences, I would merely let it go so as not to alarm my family. If any occurrence happened, I would have no choice but to inform the rest.

The night goes incredibly slow for a young boy. It is amazing how thoughts can race concerning ghosts and other things unexplained. After many hours, I saw my old friend rising in the east and felt secure again.

Of course, the first thing I did was to examine outside the window without telling a soul. There was nothing. Apparently, the creature was standing directly on our deck. I didn't care. I just wanted it gone.

For the next few days, nothing more happened. The odor was gone, and there were no more tracks to be found anywhere. I almost wanted to venture to the old burnt houses to see for myself if the creature had abandoned its post. I felt it best to leave well enough alone. Besides, I believe I would most likely have walked the path alone, and that was never going to happen. It was gone, and that's how I was going to leave it. Still, though, I could not shake the sight of the leathery face staring in through the window.

I wondered, what if I had to relieve my bowels and would have looked at it a foot away with only the screen to separate us. I knew I must not dwell upon it. I must continue to believe it was over. Looking back as an adult, though, I realized now it was only the beginning of what would be a lifetime of nightmares and fear.

Moving On

After a solid week of waiting for another visit, we all got the news that we were waiting on. There had been a sighting in the next town over. According to the local paper, people were calling it a 'walking black bear.' Without saying a word, we all just looked at each other and knew it had come to an end.

My mother broke the silence by saying, "It says here that a lady saw what the police described as a black bear walking on two legs, standing by her shed."

She continued with, "The lady saw the bear standing with its hand on the edge of the roof and then ran off."

"It can't be a coincidence," stated Al. "It must be our beast!"

Coincidence or not, all I knew was that it seemed to be moving away from us. It was finally coming to an end.

"Let's just make sure for a little while longer and keep up with what we're doing," said Dad.

No discussion and no argument. It was a first for both Al and me to be in total agreement with our parents. Life had now been miraculously put back on track, and we were heading for the summer I anticipated.

Visions of Parish's pond and fishing came streaming back and then in an instant all I could see was the face peering back at me through the thick growth of pine trees on the hill opposite my fishing spot and across the pond. I could not get that face out of my mind. I was haunted by the thought of what could be.

In an instant, my father stated, "What do you say we all take a ride to the shore today."

Normally family rides were the worst thing I wanted to hear, but today it just seemed like the right thing to do. We all began to load the family car with the accouterments needed for our outing. The familiar red and white 'Playmate' cooler stuffed with sandwiches and soda. The necessary 'boom box' radio that we always had with us and the old army blanket to stake out our piece of real estate in the sand.

It was just the diversion needed to jump start our family back to a better time. Even though we were not alone in our decision to head to the shore, we didn't even mind the traffic or the hour-long ride to reach the salty air. In fact, it seemed more enjoyable than other times and I relished the ride.

The saying, "All good things must come to an end" is, unfortunately, true. Even the peace of mind that we experienced had to finish. We ended the day with the usual stop for dinner at one of the various diners located along the New Jersey highways and headed for home.

As the family approached our destination, the silence began to take hold. I can't remember if it was the fear that we had experienced with our recent adventure or just the fact that we had become accustomed to being on alert when arriving home. It was unbearable, but we turned into our driveway, and everyone leaned forward to see what the high beam of the headlights would discover. Nothing. Just the emptiness of the dark with only our imaginations to complete the picture.

Perhaps it was finished – although there was still the chance that it would, again, come back when we were all off guard. I couldn't take the chance. I would use the bathroom before anyone went to bed, just to make sure.

There are few times in a child's life when it's known that the decision to be made ranks up with that of an adult. Staring at the window in the bathroom just filled me with dread, but it had to be done. The feeling of overcoming incredible danger bolstered my strength, and I proceeded up the stairs intact. My encounter still fresh in my mind but known only to me.

As my head sank into the pillow, all I

could do was think of what tomorrow might bring. Another encounter? Or was it over. I would see in the morning.

"Dale!" I awoke to the voice of my mother yelling up the stairs. "Breakfast is ready!"

I was down the stairs in a shot and ready to discover my answer that I had been wondering all night.

"Any sign of anything last night?" I asked.

"Yes, there was" my father replied.

I felt all the strength of my life drain from my very soul. It was back, was all I could think of. I just didn't know how much more I could accept. My mind kept reciting, *"When will it end?"*

"It looks like it was now seen in Sussex County," my Dad said.

Sussex County? That was even farther away than before. It was leaving and putting distance between our family and itself! I could almost cry at the ultimate joy!

"It says here that a farmer saw a bear on two legs reaching into a rabbit hutch and kill all of his rabbits. Upon further investigation, it was determined that the heads of the rabbits had been torn off" Dad continued as he read the paper.

I knew it, I thought. It was capable of killing, and it was also a meat eater. It was dangerous, and we were lucky to be alive. I now had the belief that it was hunting us and was only waiting for the right opportunity to strike. Now it was gone, and I would no longer have to worry.

We spent the day working around the house doing yard work. We didn't seem to mind the extra work because it felt good to do something as a family again. Even Al was beginning to do his usual complaining. That's when I knew things were getting back to normal. Even the wildlife in the forest had returned, and we began seeing deer again.

The day came and went, and we all enjoyed the usual cookout on the Hibachi grill that my father always used. It was small and could only use charcoal, but it was the part of the cookout that was interesting to watch as my father oversaw all outside cooking. The usual staple of hamburgers, hotdogs, and hot sausage went without a hitch.

After which, my father suggested a walk down the road. As I heard the words, fear began to take me until I realized that this was a necessary move to put the entire situation behind us. Even though afraid, I could not refuse to go for the mere fact that this was the conclusion necessary to end the recurring thoughts I had. I had to go.

The night air was becoming cooler, and I knew the summer was fading away. My entire family walked the neighborhood road for about a mile. Always mindful of what might lie in waiting, but nothing. I contemplated at every turn the face just staring at me and grimacing with large crooked teeth. Again, the mind of a child cannot only see the danger but also enhance it to the extreme.

We continued and listened to the symphony of the night, knowing that as long as the night creatures were out, we were safe. As we continued, the sight of our house loomed in the distance, and we were but a short distance away from the entire matter being finished. It was over. We were back, and no incident had occurred. We had survived.

We continued to resume our nightly walks and followed the sightings in the papers until the creature had continuously moved away from us. The last reported incident that we had heard of was in New York and moving north. Yes, it was officially over.

All Grown Up

The summer of my youth seems to have been a long distant memory. As I look back now as an adult with a family of my own, I almost feel that it was nothing more than a bad dream.

The thoughts of where we encountered our monster have been replaced with the familiar business of the adult. Pursuing a career and paying bills were exchanged for the kickball games and fishing at Parish's pond. Of course, in the exchange, I have also been able to enjoy the thrills of finding the woman of my dreams and the joys of fatherhood.

The career I pursued so much is now in

retirement, and I have been able to take up hobbies such as hunting and fly fishing. The price paid for adulthood came with bitterness as time stole my childhood.

I lost my father to the ravages of cancer, and my mother grew frail and elderly. Al and I have lost touch over the years due to not seeing eye to eye on certain subjects. I ran into Gooch about five months ago, and stared into his face, wondering if mine had also aged so much.

Again, I began to think of the clock in the old classroom and how I wanted it to race faster to enjoy my youth. I now realize he was only a thief of life. The clock had beaten me and continued to laugh the entire time I proceeded.

There are life changing events that take place for everyone. The day you get your driver's license. The first date you went on and how ridiculous you were dressed when you look back. The day you get married and have children. All of which are momentous occasions that bring joy and happiness. Of course, there are others that bring sadness, such as death or serious injury. Then there was my life changing incident in 1976.

I only now realize just how much it has impacted my life. Even though my wife found it silly, that I had a difficult time venturing near any forest at night, I continued to hide my devastating fear of what may lie there. The fear was merely passed on that I must be afraid of black bears, but the truth never came out.

I would also have an irrational fear of my children playing where I could not observe them. Over time, I began to believe the fear I was experiencing may have been what others were saying. I started to believe that when I went fishing or hunting, it was necessary to carry a sidearm, "just in case." Never realizing that I had suppressed the fear, I experienced in my youth and placed it deep in my subconscious.

Darkness also became a terrifying enemy that I could not cope with. I would dread having to do everyday tasks of letting out our dogs for fear of what may be lurking in the backyard. Even though the entire yard was fenced and the dogs would be let out ahead of me, it was still on my mind as to what may lie there.

I even went so far as to ensure there was some weapon available, "just in case." Perhaps that is one reason I began a career as a police officer. The security of the badge and firearm provided the protection my soul so desperately sought.

I believe I was able to suppress my fear to the point where it was manageable. I could continue with life to the best of my ability without ever compromising myself or allowing others to know what happened.

Over time I merely forgot about the summer of 1976 and replaced the memory with other reasons for my fear. It wasn't until recently I began to remember the incident because of various television programs focusing on Bigfoot. With each viewing of the television shows, I began to relive the memory of my youth and started to feel the fear I hadn't felt in so many years. The thought of gripping with the mere belief of what happened and what could still be there.

I even went so far as to try to end the irrational belief by sitting down with my family and viewing an old copy of "The Legend of Boggy Creek." Of course, I forewarned my family as to the absolute fear that such a viewing could cause.

I explained to everyone that this was an extremely scary picture and it would almost certainly cause nightmares. As the film progressed, I was met with laughter from both my daughters and wife. I thought that perhaps the laughter was to hide any fear so as not to appear silly, but this was not the case.

As the scariest part of the film began with the creature's hand reaching into the window and attempting to grab the young girl, it was met with even more laughter. My twelve-year-old daughter went so far as to say; "You can see the zipper on the monkey suit."

It was at this point that I knew I had an irrational fear that I could not control. I had to convince myself that the incident was over. I even went so far to go into my workshop in the backyard and say to myself, "It's over, let it go." It was not to be. I couldn't.

I began a quest to put the encounter behind me and went back to where it all began. Standing behind the old house, I stared at the woods edge, searching for any movement, only to see nothing. I ventured past the hedge on the edge of where the deck used to be and could still hear the breathing.

Looking through the bathroom window, I could almost see the small boy staring back at me as if I were the creature. So much time had passed. I walked up the hill, passing the old barn where Al and Gooch spent the night of investigation, now collapsing upon itself after being the casualty of a large tree.

I continued past to where the garden stood. I traced the footprints in my mind through the neatly edged rows, now replaced by a lawn and waited for a stone to land. Still nothing. I then proceeded to the top of the hill and waited on the edge of the woods and peered into the dark canopy covered theater to find it was only inhabited by a few squirrels and birds. It was over as far as I could tell. It was also soothing to know that my fear was tamed.

I still had to check the area of the burnt houses. Again, time had changed all, and the houses had been replaced by a large home with a gate. I thought, "if they only knew what happened here." I could see the power line access road in the distance only to discover it had all but disappeared in the heavy forest growth. Everything had changed and been erased so that it became difficult to even imagine where the familiar landmarks had been.

I had one more place to go that was the rock and foundation of my childhood. I had to see Parish's pond and the absolute greatest fishing spot in the world. Of course, I would not get too close to the edge because I had been told on numerous occasions by my parents, "watch out because the pond is deep." That could only mean that the pond was bottomless and if I were to slip, it was possible that my body would not be found. Again, the beliefs of a boy.

Upon arriving, I was stunned to see the pond totally dry. The edges covered in long hay and scattered broken branches. What astonished me the most was that the depth was no more than six feet. My childhood and fear were now over. I was released and had no bondage to 1976. It was over.

Camping in Lancaster, PA

Years have passed since the incident occurred and I have moved on. My family and I are avid campers and truly enjoy being outdoors. We even went so far as to purchase a 'pop-up' camper and decided to take a family vacation camping in Lancaster, Pennsylvania. It was a perfect place to visit with just the right amount of quaintness and tourism to make the trip relaxing.

We chose just the right campground, nestled between a slow-moving stream and an Amish farm. It was just what was needed to relax with my family. We discovered a long time ago that there is no other place to let go than around a campfire at night. I can still hear the horses that were directly behind us. Our camper was positioned along the double horse fence being directly behind our camper. We made sure that we were at least eight feet away so that the horses had no opportunity of reaching our canvas top.

Our stay was scheduled for a week, and there were only three campers in the campground, so we felt as if it was our private campground. It felt good to be back in nature. Everything feels so clean and alive, and we blended right in with our new surroundings.

It was our third night in the campground. We had just settled down for the night, and the campfire had only a few burning coals to show its fading life. I slept on the one slide out bed, while Lynn and my youngest daughter were on the opposite end of the camper. My oldest daughter was asleep on the converted table bed in the middle, and we were all done in. Our vacation consisted of traveling to the sights in the area, and we were all a little tired. The bunks felt good.

Our camper the morning after the incident.

Around three a.m., there was suddenly a movement outside of our camper. I awoke and stared into the darkness, trying to figure out if the horses were close by. Just then, the entire end of the camper where Lynn and our daughter were asleep, lifted off the ground by about a foot. The camper then came slamming back down. I sat up to find everyone trying to make sense out of what had just occurred.

Our first thought was a horse had leaned over and pushed on the camper. That was quickly ruled out, due to the distance between the fence and the camper. Then the thought of a prankster came to mind or perhaps a curious bear. That was enough for a check with the flashlight, and as I began to move, the camper raised again and slammed to the ground. It occurred to me then that a bear could not pick up the camper because they are incapable of rotating their wrists. It must be a prankster, but we knew no individuals around. Being that I always traveled with a pistol handy, it was found along with a strong flashlight and made ready.

With the swing of the door, we discovered nothing outside. The only thing that caught my interest was a faint smell of a decaying animal that was probably hit on the nearby road. In front of our campground, I could see the blinking of the lights of the high-tension line towers. I re-entered the camper only to discover that my entire family had to make a group trip to the facilities. I'm sure we looked ridiculous traveling in a tight group with flashlights, like search lights around us all.

The next morning, we discussed the

encounter with the desk clerk in the office. His response being, "It was either someone messing with you or a bear." This made no sense to me whatsoever. We shrugged it off and tried to continue with our little vacation.

It wasn't until later that we discovered a very large Bigfoot sighting area around Lancaster. I pushed the incident out of mind and got on with our vacation with no further incidences.

A Picnic Encounter

I have officially retired from my second career of construction and my wife, and I have decided to take matters into our own hands. Lynn and I decided that we were not fully satisfied with the public-school system and we began to homeschool our two daughters. Even though this is a daunting task, to say the least, we still believed that it would be better for all and we began.

We pulled our kids out of school and began a whirlwind of learning and field trips. For history, we decided it was better to live history than to read about it and we all became re-enactors for various time periods. Science became very hands on, along with

129

other subjects and we became stronger as a family.

To ease the transition from school to home, we would often take picnics at various locations around our home. I had now impressed myself with the knowledge that there was nothing in the woods that could ever hurt us because the forest creatures would always run away when humans were present. Bears were not a threat because I was never afraid of them and besides, I had hunted and became familiar with seeing them from time to time. The past was in the past, and I had only the future to look at now.

We all decided that the day was perfect for a picnic at Chad Park. It was a recreation park that was well known for 4H Fairs and carnivals, not to mention that people played on the tennis courts and soccer fields for the best part of the year. It was just the place for fried chicken and relaxing.

Packing our supplies reminded me of the times my family would go to the Jersey shore and all the preparations that we would make for such an outing. I could still see the familiar red and white cooler and couldn't help but think of my father being replaced by myself. It was now our time to make memories, and this was a great way to. We sped on our way with our cargo and a familiar tune on the radio. I think we were all looking forward to our outing to relax and cut loose a little.

Upon arrival at Chad Park, it was clear to see that the public school was in session because of the lack of people in the park. In fact, there were only a few other cars as we pulled in and we immediately went over and scouted a picnic table in a secluded little grove of trees near the playground.

We laughed as we enjoyed the crisp fried chicken and iced tea we brought. Of course, mom's iced tea was still the best, but this made a suitable substitute. We finished our lunch, and the girls decided to check out the playground to see what there was to do. Being that we were just enjoying the day and being outdoors, there was no school work to do.

As lunch ended, Lynn stated; "How

about we go for a hike? The day is beautiful, and it's so pretty here."

"I think that sounds like a great idea" I replied.

"Let's just put the leftovers in the car because we don't want anything getting into them," Lynn·answered.

So, we packed up the remainders and gathered our children for a warm nature hike. There were trails just behind the ball fields and tennis courts with paved walkways leading us through the woods.

As we entered the woods, I couldn't help but feel a slight twinge of the past, but shrugged it off as childish memories that had no room in my future. We continued down shady paths until, suddenly, the feeling of too much iced tea became evident and I knew what must be done.

Further down the hill, I noticed a small access road that followed the power lines and crossed our very path. I knew this was my chance to rectify the situation and announced that I had to make a pit stop.

Of course, that was met with scowls of

"Really Dad?" from all three of the ladies in my life. I rebuffed their complaints and proceeded down the small access road. Of course, I surveyed my environment to be sure there were no unwanted eyes that could be upon me. I found just the right bush with the amount of privacy I desired to make my task possible. Thank goodness, the park was almost empty because I was sure, on any given day; I would not have been able to get away with what I was about to do.

I entered a bushy area and began my task when Lynn suddenly announced;

"Do you smell that?"

I breathed in a long breath to try to detect any smoke of what I thought would be, perhaps, someone smoking and walking the paths with us. The scent that permeated my nostrils returned me to another time. I finished only to discover we were not alone on the paths. The rotting acrid smell of the past was back, but now it was in the presence of my family.

I retreated from my private bush only to discover the bushes approximately fifty feet away began to violently shake from side to side. The smell was now everywhere and getting stronger. It was back and became as real as a thundering train overtaking me.

As my family became aware of what was happening, we all began to back up the hill as fast as possible to get away without incident. It was then that our intruder made itself known with a terrifying scream that would have made any bear run in fear. We continued up the hill, and I frantically searched the ground as we did so, for any weapon I might be able to find. I convinced myself that any attack would result in me fighting to the death to save my wife and children.

Staring into my family's eyes, I could easily see the fear that was gripping them. We continued up the hill and desperately tried to get as much distance between us and *it*. As we moved up, the intruder was paralleling our every move. I knew it was only a matter of time before it would no longer be satisfied with watching and would act.

Our future seemed dim until I heard a

motor approaching. As I sped around, there was a utility power truck driving down the paved pathway. It was the perfect opportunity to escape because the vehicle had now put itself between us and the creature and I was sure it would force the beast to retreat. It was our chance for us to move and get away intact.

The top of the hill could not come fast enough. I concerned myself with not only the safety of my children but also Lynn's health. She suffered from asthma that could become so severe; she would be hospitalized from time to time. I scanned her breathing as we arrived at the woods edge and determined she needed her inhaler. We progressed passed the tennis courts and found the safety of our car and her medication.

Out of breath, tired and a little scared, the past flooded back to my mind and felt grateful to hear the motor turn over again. As we sped off for home, we all discussed what had just happened, and my family finally understood what had gripped me my whole life. There was no laughter anymore about my past, only a deep understanding as to why.

We sped home convinced that it was all about to begin again. When we arrived home, all we could talk about was what had just taken place. Questions were focused on me as to what happened in my childhood and what we would do now. My only response was that, as in the past, we were now at the mercy of something we could not openly see.

As my girls requested to know what was to come, my only answer was, "I don't know."

The Nightmare Continues

lmost a year has passed since the incident at the park. I was, again haunted by the events that came streaming back from the past. I have searched for answers as to why this continues to occur around me and have ruled out completely any level of coincidence.

It has been brought to my attention that there could be some connection to my direct Native American heritage, but I don't know. I have sought the help of others as to ways to prevent any further sightings and have found none. Just when I believe the events are over, another reminder becomes evident. On occasion, as distant smells at night or

137

sightings by neighbors. It continues to plague me.

We have recently decided to move to Pennsylvania and secretly in the back of my mind; I believe that it could be a new start to put everything behind us and move on. I know this is just me trying to rationalize the situation. I continued to struggle with my fear until one day; I was watching the movie, "The Great Gatsby," with my family and during the film, it was discussed by one of the characters that, "If you want to get it out of your mind, write it down."

Lynn urged me to write down the story because it was an important part of our family history.

I had to admit; it did relieve my fear tremendously, and now I can cope with my thoughts of the past. I don't believe I will ever get over it, but I can deal with the thought much more comfortably.

I have learned much more about the questions I have had. I did learn that sightings of such a creature have taken place for hundreds of years and by prominent members of society. I now know I'm not alone.

In fact, as I was investigating my experience, I had the opportunity to speak with people who also saw my beast in 1976. I have had the privilege of speaking with eyewitnesses and developed a solid friend base of what could be construed as 'survivors'. There are more of us than one would think.

I did make some discoveries that I would like to pass on that might make sense of what happened to me. The parallel I discovered in the 1976 incidences, the camping trip and the later encounter in the park, both stemmed around the power lines. I have discovered that many sightings occur around power lines because if you were to look at the area itself, it almost resembles a natural highway, cut through the forest for miles.

During the park encounter, I had urinated in the woods. Unfortunately, I believe the beast believed that I was encroaching on its territory and in nature, dominant males often urinate to warn others of boundary lines. I do believe that even though there are numerous people that believe the creature would be docile, I truly believe that there is no way of positively knowing how a true encounter would result.

I am respectful of where the boundary lines exist and have no intention of intruding into the domain of such a creature. Even though I do enjoy activities such as hunting, fishing, and camping, I am still very mindful of my surroundings and continue, to this day, to carry a firearm when traversing in the woods. I encourage everyone to understand that these creatures do exist and have existed for hundreds of years in recorded history.

Native Americans and Original Peoples around the world have always been aware of these creatures. As I watch numerous television shows on the investigation of such, I can't help but believe that it's in mankind's interest to just avoid them. I have spent a lifetime trying to avoid them and have failed. I wish only to live a normal life.

I have recently discovered that where I am moving in Pennsylvania, is close to the second highest Bigfoot sighting area in the United States. Therefore, as I finish my story, I know it's only part of what will come. I am sure that if the past is indicative of the future, my story is not yet finished. I only hope it will end with me and not continue to my family.

I was recently asked if I could give any advice as to the existence of such a creature. My answer was, "Believe."

Spending a lifetime as I did was no way to live. Be mindful of your surroundings and understand that you are never alone. I believe it's a matter of time before mankind encounters these 'beings' head on. I can only hope that such a meeting will not end in tragedy.

I am aware that there will always be people that are curious and wish to have their own encounter, but the best advice I can give is to avoid this temptation.

In the past, I have been asked to go on Bigfoot Hunts in hopes that my connection to these creatures may lead to an encounter that may be documented. After every request, my mind wanders back to a lost summer and the stolen memories of a little boy. As my thoughts begin to clear, my answer remains the same every time;

"Thank you, but I think I will pass."

ABOUT THE AUTHOR

A.H. Verge was originally born on a dairy farm in Westfield, VT. He currently resides in Eastern Pennsylvania and is the founder of the Tego Tea Company, a Native American tea that is currently being examined to reduce the effects of Diabetes. He is passionate about his Native Ancestral heritage and continues to enjoy a rich, fulfilled life in the outdoors with his family and friends.

Please leave a review on Amazon. I really want to hear what you think about my terrifying experience when I was a boy just looking forward to a summer of fun.

Thank you
A.H. Verge

And now on with the next adventure.

Coming soon to Amazon

The Little Englishman

…based on the true story of my great, great grandfather Edward's extraordinary life after stowing away on a ship from England to the New World when he was only seven years old. A tale of hardship, perseverance, and coming of age in a frontier world.

Chapter 1

"Edward", I could hear my mother say as I slowly began to wake. I could feel the warm touch of the sun's kiss upon my cheek and the familiar rustle of my mother's dress. "It's time to get up Edward," she softly stated. As my eyes began to focus, I could see the room as it was, with the stark white walls and meager furnishings. We were not considered rich, but by no means were we to be thought of as poor.

My father was a prosperous merchant near the waterfront and we lived not far from the view of the tall ship's masts in the distance. England in 1849 was a bustling hub, where ships from the America's and beyond were continuously venturing in and out of port.

Walking along the cavalcade of ships was a favorite for me as a seven-year-old boy. The treasures from far away lands could be obtained along the docks and was sometimes purchased when my father joined us in our jaunts.

My mother was my entire world. I can see her in her white and blue dress with the small blue flowers. The same dress that less than a week ago I had pressed my face into so deeply, when I had become frightened in the previous nights dreams and needed her care. Her long flowing brown hair, neatly tucked inside a bonnet, presented her in pure elegance. I loved my mother so and by the way she held me in her arms afforded me the protection and care that every small boy cherishes.

"We will be visiting your father today at the market, so let's wash and dress so that we may leave soon," she stated. My clothing was adequate for a boy my age. The short pants and matching jacket were of course the clothing I was allotted for church, but being that we were going to market, the upgrade was so warranted. My shoes were neatly placed under my bed and were poised at the ready. Unlike other children of my age, I had two pairs of shoes. My first pair was worn to within uselessness, while the other pair was for church and special occasions. I looked forward to our market days when we could dress to our fullest and look our best. Perhaps the onlookers would stare at my mother and me as usual and smile. They would sometimes whisper after we had passed. I had asked my mother why they did such and she confided that father was "prominent." The starched, white linen shirt neatly tucked into my short pants. The small, black cravat, tied in the perfect bow beneath my chin. "We were prominent," I thought.

As we began our journey, I can feel the uneven stone of the cobble street as we pass along the numerous store fronts and various shops on our way to the wharf. My mother's hand wrapped softly around my own to give me the strength and love I did so enjoy. As I glanced up toward her, her eyes gazed down upon my face with the pure bond that only a mother and child could know. We continued to walk and smiled at the various people that passed by. I had the feeling that perhaps we were part of the Royal family, strolling by our subjects along our designated route. As we came closer to the waterfront, I could not help but notice the disheveled men that were scurrying about. Perhaps they did not have the same life that had been chosen for me, or perhaps they enjoyed not looking their best. It was of no difference to me because I was proper and clean and did not have to gaze upon the likes of this sort.

"Here we are Edward", my mother said. Unknowingly we had arrived at our destination. Mother would collect the harvest needed for everyday life from the local merchants and afterwards we would spend time with father. Being that the market was along the waterfront, I had to stay within close proximity to my mother. I was never allowed to go near the ships without the protection of my father. I had been told that many of the sailors were of the "unsavory kind" and would take great delight in snatching a boy if the chance were given.

"Mother" I asked? "May I walk through

the market?" I loved to create my own adventure and possibly look at the ships from a distance. The thought of pirates and other scoundrels always filled my mind with fear and delight.

"Yes my dear Edward but remember not to venture far", my mother replied.

I was amazed at the numerous languages being spoken that I could not understand. It was pure delight and added to my imagination of how excitement could be around every corner. I could still see my mother in the distance, inspecting produce. I passed by a poulterer with numerous cages of fowl ready to be purchased and noticed an older boy staring at me. He was dressed shabbily for the market and I could see he was not like me. He spat upon the ground when I looked upon him and I knew that he held disdain for me. The gaze that he focused upon me began to terrorize me into thinking that perhaps this boy would harm me or worse, he would soil my perfect clothing. I continued on my path, trying to avoid his glance but noticed he had begun to follow me through the marketplace. I continued past the large piles of fabric, trying to put some distance between us and discovered that his numbers were increasing. He had recruited two other boys and they were all tracking me through the crowd. I now realized that these boys had "chased" me away from the safety of my mother and were pushing me closer to the ships.

The fear now grew in me to the point that I realized I had to escape before the group could catch me. I glanced over my shoulder to discover the numbers had grown to six. I had to escape but had been now blocked in. I was able to evade my pursuers thus far but it was only a matter of time before they would find me. I could see that whatever their reasoning could be, it surely was not good for me.

I squatted down amongst merchandise and glanced up to find my pursuers. They were closing in and I had no choice but to run. My first option would have been for me to return to my mother, but that was out of the question. I had no choice but to run toward the ships. As I arose to make my escape, my position was revealed and all six began chase. I immediately ran up the gang plank onto one of the ships and across the deck. I glanced back and the boys were following up the plank. With no other place of escape, I ran down into the belly of the ship for a place to hide.

All at once I heard the yell of a deep voiced man on deck. In an instant, I could tell by the departure of footsteps that my pursuers had fled and left only the ranting of the deep voiced man, shouting in a foreign language. I was safe. I would only have to go topside and run off the ship myself and back to my waiting family.

The hold where I was hiding was very dark and filled with numerous crates and debris. I could barely make out the exit when suddenly I heard more voices on deck. Men were coming on board and by the number of footsteps, there were many. I realized that I had to exit the ship now before it was too late. I would go topside and try to explain why I had come aboard and the reasoning for such. I was sure that once the men realized how I was dressed, they would understand and allow me to exit. I began to emerge from my hiding space only to come face to face with another. He was a thin man, with a filthy face and he was staring at me from behind another crate. I stopped in pure fear and watched as he slowly withdrew a knife from his side. He just stared at me and motioned for me to be quiet. I could hear the men scurrying about the deck and loud clanging noises above. I stood motionless with my intruder just an arms length away. As I began to slowly rise, he only pointed at me with the knife point and instructed me to return to my seat.

Along the wharf, my mother began to search the merchants for her missing joy. There was no sign of little Edward anywhere. As she ventured from one merchant to another, the outcome was the same. Edward was not to be found anywhere among the crowds. Panic began to ensue and the search became frantic. "Edward!" she screamed. "Where are you?" No reply could be heard from any direction. "Edward!" she shrieked again. Still nothing could be heard. At that moment, my father came running for he had heard that his little man had gone missing. The pair ran up and down the pier shrieking "Edward, where are you?"

I could hear my mother and father both screaming outside and knew that it would only take one scream to re-join them. As I drew in the breath to perform my task, my adversary slid forward on his knees and pressed the tip of the blade to my chest. Normally I would have become upset with the thought of the un-clean instrument possibly damaging my little coat but now I stopped for fear of the blade piercing my chest. "Edward?" again came screeching across the wharf. I had to take my chance before all hope was lost and I addressed my opponent by saying in a soft voice "I am Edward." The man only smiled with a mouth filled with rotting teeth and started to laugh, motioning me to remain quiet and seated. My fear of not finding my parents was excruciating. I began to cry and plead with the man to please allow me to leave and he only pressed the point deeper into my chest. I could hear the cry for my return getting dimmer. I could do nothing. I only sat on the hard decking crying in my urine soaked short pants.

Suddenly I felt my surroundings heave to one side and realized my absolute worst fears were happening. The ship was leaving port. I heard my mother's voice, scream in a frantic effort to locate me and decided that I must leave now. I stood up in defiance and was abruptly knocked to the floor by the filthy man. As I lie there on the boards with my cheek resting on years of grime, I heard the sound of my mother's voice for the last time followed by the sobbing a woman would make at the death of her own. My vision began to fade as the feeling of liquid flowed down across my face. "Mother", was the last word that escaped from my mouth.

Coming soon to Amazon

SPECIAL LINKS

www.facebook.com/NightmareInTheWoods/

https://www.tegotea.com/

Made in the USA
San Bernardino, CA
29 August 2019